Ocean of Light

30 years in Tonga and the Pacific

Other books by Peter Warner

Ocean of Light: 30 years in Tonga and the Pacific, 1st edn, 2016.

ASTOR: adventures ashore and afloat, 2018.

Ocean of Light

30 years in Tonga and the Pacific

Peter R. Warner

Connor Court Publishing

Second Edition Published by
Connor Court Publishing, 2020

© Peter Raymond Warner 2018, 2020

Connor Court Publishing Pty Ltd
PO BOX 7257, Redland Bay, QLD, 4165

First edition published by Peter Raymond Warner
Keerrong, NSW 2480, Australia, 2018.

Edited by Yvonne I. Woźniak
Original images amended by Michael W. Thomas

Front cover: Section of Australasia and Adjacent Waters map,
Int 60, Aus 4060, Commonwealth of Australia, 1992.

ISBN: 9781925826999

Contents

Dedication

This book is dedicated to my children and grandchildren, grand nieces and nephews and all their descendants. I hope it will help you to appreciate where I am coming from, and how I gradually came to understand the world in the way I now do through my old eyes.

Life has taught me many things including the notion of always looking for the good and positive things in people—i.e. their moral and spiritual virtues.

So this book, which is really a study of interesting and intriguing people set in romantic and wild backgrounds, will start you thinking about their virtues; and how and for what purpose were all these people placed on this planet.

All your endeavours, including reading, should be a joyful experience. I have tried to make the book entertaining, but with a hidden lesson or two imbedded in some cases. This was an early trick of Walt Disney. You always thought his cartoons were entertaining you, but there was a moral lesson concealed in the stories. This does not always register immediately. It is called "sugar coated education", and is used extensively in the teaching profession.

Throughout this book, you will also see examples of lateral thinking—a talent that you may already be blessed with or that you may develop in yourselves. Everybody in this world must learn to be adaptable to situations and circumstances. The King of Tonga once said to me, "Peter, we must learn to be like pussy cats." Naturally, I was puzzled by this strange comment and asked:

"Why Your Majesty"?

"Well", said the King, "have you ever noticed that when you throw a cat in the air, it always lands on its feet!" So please note how the survivors in this book, including myself, have learned to be adaptable and land on our feet.

Acknowledgements

Much help from many people was needed in preparing this book for its first edition. The greatest effort was made by Joye Spink, my dear neighbour and talented artist, who created the graphic design and layout. Assisting her with the first edit was her sister Alana. Later a friend of my daughter Janet, a kindly and professional copy editor, Judy Renouf undertook the final edit.

Bill Cole, who was with me from the start of Warner Pacific Line, jolted my memory, edited my text on shipping, and sourced many of the ship illustrations.

Justine and Carolyn, my dear wife and daughter, corrected my spelling and edited the worst of my grammar. They also toned down some of my irritating claims.

'Evelini Faletau, family friend and the widow of my good mate, the late Honourable 'Akau'ola, corrected many items in the chapters concerning the Tongan royal family and The Eccentric Crown Prince. 'Evelini's daughter, Mele Vikatolia Faletau, had the privilege to serve HRH Crown Prince Tupouto'a as his personal secretary. She has provided additional insight, and cherished anecdotes of her late boss. Some of her photos have been invaluable and her efforts are much appreciated. Mele is a highly reliable source of information on the Royal family. Not only was she married to the late nephew of His majesty Tupou IV—and consequently is now the mother of HSH Prince Tu'ipelehake—but also, as a young lady, Mele gained the highest honours at Oxford in the dead languages of Ancient Greek and Latin.

Lessons from the Bahá'í Faith gifted me with the insight and inspiration to undertake this satisfying but big task of composing a story with a message. The late Grenville Kirton, the Bolouri family, and my spiritual mentors Ghodrat and Sima Motalebi, together with Camel and Khosrow Lalehzari, inspired me and charged my spiritual batteries with the knowledge needed to produce this book.

Typographical and other errors, which crept into the text of the first edition before printing, are in no way the fault of the original editors. Hopefully, these have all been corrected in this revised second edition—edited, formatted, images enhanced, and prepared for publishing by my Bahá'í friends, Yvonne Woźniak and Michael Thomas.

Foreword

Dear Reader

My name is Sione Filipe Totau, known to all my relatives and friends as Mano. I was one of the six Tongan teenagers who the author of this book, Peter Warner found castaway on the uninhabited of island of ATA about 50 years ago. Read about it in chapter one of this book.

Thank God, both Peter and I are still alive over 50 years later. Over these many years, our friendship has had its ups and downs. Peter was not happy with me when I wrecked his beloved boat "Just David". But our very long friendship has deepened over time as we both became wiser. I have learned all his bad ways and he knows all my bad ways so we understand each other very well.

In a way, he was like a teacher and supported me like a comforting uncle in my wildest days. We still have long talks about my favorite subject the Bible. I am now an ordained minister of the Christian Church known as the "Assembly of God". I read the Bible every day in both Tongan and English. Even though Peter has moved from a foundation in Christianity to the Baha'i Faith, he still admits the Bible is the word of God, even if he interprets some of it differently to me. So we have much to talk about on this subject. I think I know more about it than him.

Justine Warner, Peter's real boss and supportive wife was the first to teach me the basics of European type cooking which helped me when I became a chef and managed a French restaurant in Tonga. But I like better working closer to nature, planting and fishing rather than cooking. That's why I still grow vegetables and root crops at home in Brisbane.

Peter's family has been close to my large family and it is a pleasure, at my age, to still work seasonally with Peter looking after nut growing orchards. This keeps us busy and healthy touching and smelling the earth and nature close at hand. We agree that any type of work which is a service to mankind is much better than just talking about it.

I hope you enjoy reading this book which Peter has been working on for about 16 years. It's a good story with great lessons buried in it.

Sione Filipe Totau, 2018

Introduction

This is the second edition of Part 2 of my autobiography. As it covers the most interesting part of my life on this planet, I decided to publish it in 2016 before Parts 1 and 3 were finished because, at the age of 85, I felt that my time might be running out. Now, with Part 1 recently published under the title of *ASTOR: adventures ashore and afloat*, I decided to publish a new corrected edition of *Ocean of Light*, while I continue working on Part 3.

The title *Ocean of Light* embraces both spiritual and physical connotations. There is no doubt that the Pacific Ocean and especially the tropical parts are bright, both day and night. Most times, majestic twilights of the dawn (*ata mai Langi*) herald bright blue skies and deep blue azure seas. Evening twilight foreshadows a clear and intense flood of bright planets, stars—and now also satellites—that illuminate the dark heavens. On moonless nights, when adrift at sea, flashes of bright green phosphorescence trace the movement of life in the black but clear deep water below. Tropical dark nights afloat on a calm sea provide the illusion of being suspended in a dark void between two sources of light above and below. These are the physical aspects that stimulate the imaginations of all who witness this vast canvas of nature

There is an excellent school in Tonga called the Ocean of Light International School. There is a chapter in this book devoted to it. Many ask why this name was chosen for a primary and secondary school. The names for the school and this book were chosen for the same spiritual reason. The great-grandson of the Co-Founder of the Bahá'ís was appointed as "Guardian" of the Faith in the Will and Testament of his Grandfather.

The Guardian encouraged pioneers to spread the light of this young Faith to as many earthly places as possible. By the time of the Guardian's death in faraway England, and as a result of a 10-year crusade that he had instigated, the light of the faith had spread throughout the Pacific to thousands of followers in 310 locations. In a moment when the Guardian's heart overflowed with gratitude for the blessings of this remarkable achievement, he described the Pacific area as the "Ocean of Light", referring to the new spiritual illumination revealed and expanding in this part of the planet.

While my autobiography was initially intended for my children and their descendants, Part 2, *Ocean of Light*, will be of particular interest to the Bahá'ís and many of my other friends. Part 1, *ASTOR: adventures ashore and afloat*, which covers my childhood, my parents—especially the doings of my impressive father, Arthur George Warner—my schooling and early youth, will be of particular interest to those with a taste for history and a yen for the sea. Part 3, *Twilight of the Dawn*, deals with my return to Australia, an aborted trial retirement, and the start of a new profession with other interests. As one grows older, maturity and wisdom develop together, so *Twilight of the Dawn* reflects a more observant, deeper and philosophical approach to this life and the next.

Meanwhile, I hope that readers will get as much enjoyment out of this little book as I did in writing it.

Peter Warner

Australia 2018

1
Forgotten island of 'Ata

1
Forgotten island of 'Ata

This episode in my life started a reaction within me, which slowly changed my perception of the journey we take on this planet, and caused me to rethink the purpose of life.

To summarize, the following anecdote covers the survival of six mischievous teenagers. Having drifted from Tongatapu for eight days in an open boat, which they wrecked on the island of 'Ata, they eked out a precarious existence for two years on this remote uninhabited rock until their discovery by my crew and me after they had all been given up as dead.

The island of 'Ata lies 90 miles south of the main island of Tongatapu. The Kingdom of Tonga itself is made up of two parallel chains of islands that stretch for more than 200 miles north and south in the South West Pacific. In 1966, 'Ata was the southernmost island in the group, but two other artificial islands were added later. Those are described in another chapter about Minerva Reef.

The reason for my voyaging in this part of the Pacific was a never-ending search for more crayfish. While still in Australia, I had maintained a small fishing enterprise in Tasmania, which, in reality, was an occasional and joyous escape from my unfulfilling shore job. Crayfish were becoming scarce off Tasmania, and our boats were forced further offshore each year to find a legitimate catch. Consequently, during each annual closed season, we mounted voyages of discovery in the South Pacific to find new crayfishing grounds. Although tropical crayfish are a different species to those of colder waters, they are of the same family, and our unquestioning US customers were happy to eat "rock lobster tails" from anywhere.

On a previous voyage (on the schooner *Astor*), we had discovered rewarding numbers of crayfish off the island of Rapa, south of Tahiti. However, on seeking a fishing license from the French in Tahiti, I was told to either register a company owned more than 50% by Frenchmen or marry a local lady, and register the venture in her name. I liked the latter suggestion but I was already happily married.

Discovery

In the winter of 1966, we fitted out *Just David*, a seaworthy 45 foot wooden fishing boat, with all the instruments and traps (pots) needed to lure crayfish. With a complement of experienced skippers and crews from our little fleet and a Sydney friend, Peter Currie, we sailed from Hobart to search the many underwater mountains stretching from the North of New Zealand to the south of Tonga.

FV *Just David* **departing Constitution Dock, Hobart 1966**

After leaving Auckland, we met a severe low with gale force winds about 28 degrees south, which forced us to drift stern towards the wind for two very uncomfortable days with streamed sea anchor, and with a punctured oil drum in the self-draining cockpit to spread an oil slick. This worked to break up the mountainous and crashing waves that had been threatening to poop us.

After the wind eased, we proceeded to some potential crayfish grounds, and tried our traps with the most enticing bait but without results other than a few octopus who entrapped themselves. We made landfall at the rocky and uninhabited island of 'Ata, and launched our traps on an underwater mountain peak about five miles to the east of the island early one sunny morning in August 1966. Whilst we were waiting for results, I trained my binoculars towards the distant green cliffs of the island, which rose sheer from the indigo blue of the deep tropical ocean.

On the tropical green cliffs there appeared to be some large burned out patches of black. It is unusual for a bush fire to start up by itself in the wet and humid tropics, and yet the island was reported to be uninhabited. I checked the relevant "Pacific Pilot", which confirmed that the uninhabited island, 700 foot high and covered in trees, is three miles long and without an anchorage.

The stone face of 'Ata Island

Other historical accounts we had on-board advised that Abel Tasman had sailed past in the 16th century and named this seemingly uninhabited island "Pijlstaart Island" because of the many thousands of frigate birds that nest there and spread their arrow-like tails. These reminded Tasman of arrows, or *pijlstaart* in Dutch. Tasman may have been mistaken about the lack of inhabitants who could have hidden themselves very well from his passing ship. Later reports said that

5

there was a small village of Tongans living in the fertile hollow of the old volcanic crater on the top of the island.

However, in the 18th century, "black birders" or pirates in search of strong cheap labourers enticed most of the male population on board one or more vessels and sailed away with them, never to be seen again. The then King of Tonga decided it was untenable for the women and children to remain alone and removed them all to the island of 'Eua where their descendants can be found today. Thereafter, the King decreed 'Ata taboo and no one was to live or even visit this uninviting spot, with its sheer cliffs, and with no surrounding coral reef and no anchorage.

In 1966, I did not know all this—or anything much at all about Tonga, its history, its people or its geography. However, I did know that it was the only Polynesian Kingdom, which had retained its internal independence from any European power. Consequently, it appeared to be master of its own destiny—at least to the extent that any nation can remain totally independent in this global community.

After recovering our empty cray pots, we decided to have a closer look and investigate the burned out patches on this stark steep-to island. We approached the eastern face first and then rounded the northern corner to investigate the western leeside. Everywhere thick clouds of screaming seabirds of all types swirled around the cliffs and over our small vessel.

Suddenly, from the crow's nest, our lookout called out, "I can hear a human voice yelling!"

"Nonsense," said I, "it's only screaming seabirds," as we steamed slow ahead.

Next moment we spotted a brown body hurtling down a cliff path and diving into the surf. He looked wild and screamed loudly, making bloodcurdling noises. With no clothes at all, and hair grown into a huge black top-heavy "gollywog" bush, this apparently healthy youngster swam towards us using the Australian crawl now known as "freestyle".

I ordered the crew to load the rifles below and stand by to repel boarders because by now a few more brown figures were seen swimming towards us. My first thoughts were that this place must be some sort of prison island for desperate Tongan thugs and outcasts. Exile was a common practice in Polynesia, with miscreants often being sent off in a leaky canoe.

However, after his Olympic-winning swim from the shore, the youth with the exploded hairdo beamed a big pearly white smile from the water alongside the boat, which calmed my nerves. We lowered the boarding ladder; and the 18-year-old heaved himself aboard, stark naked, and announced in perfect aristocratic English, "My name is Steven. There are six of us and we estimate we have been here between one and two years."

'Good story!' thought I, 'but I don't believe it!' Meanwhile the others had boarded and introduced themselves while we continued to drift and I continued to think. Even if they were all young jailbirds, we did not wish to scare them.

Their explanation continued. They alleged that five of them had come from the Ha'apai group of islands in Tonga, where fish is a staple diet; but they had been sent as boarders to St Andrew's Anglican high school in Nuku'alofa, the capital of Tonga. According to the boys, the food at the school was so horrible that they had "borrowed" a long boat one evening and sailed out to catch some fish. Having lost sight of Nuku'alofa and already far out to sea, they had drifted for eight days before finding the uninhabited island.

This was the official story that they all stuck to, for the time being. Details of this eight-day survival trip were explained to us during the first night they slept on FV *Just David*.

But first, we had to consider what to do with six dripping and very healthy boys in the after cockpit. We figured that if their story was indeed true, it sounded as if they had indeed spent between 18 months and two years on the island. However, still feeling suspicious, I wrote down the names of the six with spelling help from them. Then I raised Nuku'alofa Radio on short wave and, after sorting out a working frequency, asked the shore operator to contact St Andrew's College by phone and ask the staff if they had the six named boys as old students.

The Tongan radio operator asked me to stand-by whilst he investigated. Meanwhile our cook had prepared our daily meal, which the boys shared with us and immediately vomited up, not being used to European-style food for so long.

A very emotional and tearful Nuku'alofa Radio operator came back on the air and announced that St Andrew's College confirmed that five of the six named boys had been students at the school. They all had been given up as dead long ago when the missing boat never returned. One father had spent months looking for them on uninhabited islands but finally resigned himself to their disappearance. Funeral services for all six boys had been held; and now, miraculously, we had found them alive and very healthy!

We all relaxed, unloaded the firearms, and gave some clothes to our new friends. A temporary anchorage was found and we resolved that, next day, we would sail to Nuku'alofa. But first, we were to be given a guided tour of their island refuge, and that night we listened to the story of the eight-day drift.

Some of the castaways in FV *Just David*'s wheelhouse with me at the helm

**Rowing ashore at 'Ata, with FV *Just David*
in the background and a thrown fish in mid-air**

2
Eight days adrift and two years lost

2
Eight days adrift and two years lost

The youngest member of this gang of six impressionable schoolboys was only 13 years old and the eldest 16 years old when this adventure started. From our own life's experience, we know that the teenage years manifest the most violent, curious, defiant and adventurous stage of our existence.

These boys were no different! Like all Tongan children, their pre-youth or pre-puberty years had been well disciplined within the village system where respect is given to religious leaders, uncles, aunts and all elders. Biological parents are not so close to their own children because of a common practice of farming out their early upbringing to older relatives where the children experience the security always available and given by a loving extended family. Nevertheless, a strict pecking order prevails. Hymns and prayers are a daily part of life, and sitting still in church on Sunday is an obligation.

Living close to nature on a small island that relies on fish, root crops and water brings an early understanding of and closeness to nature's wonders. It is true that they lived in material poverty, but all churches taught that the abject would inherit spiritual rewards. It is no wonder, then, that the gang of six relied on their strong spiritual beliefs to pilot them through their adventure.

I have noticed in my long life that people facing imminent death fall back on instinctive defences, including imbedded spiritual beliefs, customs and dogma. Examples can be seen amidst today's self-destructive Arab and Persian turmoil.

Whether these boys were spiritual beings having a physical experience or physical beings having a spiritual experience, their spiritual strength played a large part in their survival.

Travel to boarding school from their home island was a 100-mile voyage in an open sailing cutter. They could all swim before they could walk and the fury of the sea was nothing new, except on moonless nights when good or evil spirits may have been present. When they

13

reached puberty and went off to boarding school, growing aggression and revolt posed new problems. So the gang of six was formed and united to better pursue their plans and execute their plots. Most of the boys were related in one way or another so unity was natural. Because of his age, size and religious fervour, one of the two eldest, Sione Fataua, became the moral leader.

Like most people, Tongans crave for strong and just leadership. Later, Steven (Fatai Latu), the other older youth, became the practical leader in physical "hands on" matters that required an innovative and inventive approach. This combination of leadership worked well as we shall see.

Every gang needs a jester, and the younger and smaller boy Kolo Fekitoa won this position. He also posed as the gang's musician. He was, indeed, the best singer in the gang. The remaining delinquents will be introduced as the story unfolds.

The rebellious gang of five did not like high school, the food or the teachers. The half-year or mid-year exams were imminent and some of the gang thought they had little chance of passing. They all hungered for better food in the form of fish. They only had protein once a week at the school and lived mainly on a diet of root crops. Deeply unhappy, they plotted to run away. Without a compass or other aids, they decided to "borrow" a boat and sail downwind to Fiji or, at the worst, catch a few fish and return with a big haul for the school kitchen.

To attempt to sail in an open boat of doubtful condition from Tonga to Fiji (400 miles) as adults is a dangerous proposition; and for teenagers, it is either heroic or stupid. It does however demonstrate the virtues of confidence, enthusiasm, faithfulness, self-discipline, courage and determination, latent within them, which were now to be tested. It seems that the boys had been inspired by the stories of brave Tongan warriors of the mid-18th century.

When early missionaries persuaded the Tongans to halt their manly pursuits of killing one another on their islands, the fierce warriors started to carry their exploits further afield. They would board their high-speed 80-foot long, double-hulled sailing canoes (*kalia*) and run before the wind from Tongatapu to the easternmost Fiji Islands (Lau group) in 24 hours. There they would burn a few villages, rape a few women; and, then, on the starboard tack, "tight reach" back to the north of Tonga, accomplishing the total voyage in about 72 hours.

Typical longboat similar to the one "borrowed" by the teenagers

Now, with their hearts fortified by the tales of their fearsome forebears, the young miscreants prepared to set out on their adventure. In Nuku'alofa harbour, the boys found a 24-foot long double-ended boat with oars and rudder, moored off the beach opposite a graveyard.

Such a boat would ground at low tide and float over the reef at high tide. It was fitted with a Tongan anchor in the form of a bag of sand on a rope, which also acted as movable ballast. All that was needed were a few provisions, easily supplied with two sacks of green bananas, a saucepan of cooked taro and a Primus stove, all loaded together with the fishing gear. A mast and sails found rolled up on the shore also disappeared with the boys in the darkness.

At high tide on a moonless night, skirting the graveyard, the six adventurers loaded up and sailed out into the starlit phosphorous sea. The weather was fine as they slipped past the light on the outer reef of Hakau Mamoa.

Once they reached the open ocean, the weather turned nasty. Very strong gusts blew out the two sails and high seas broke over the boat, which needed constant bailing. With the last Tongan island of Hunga still in sight, the rudder broke away and an oar was rigged to steer the boat downwind in the heavy seas.

Mano, of whom we will hear plenty, became the sturdy young helmsmen standing in the stern of the boat with two hands on the steering oar as they surfed down the following seas. But he was not strong enough to control the antics of the boat when it decided to skid broadside to the waves and broach. Whilst trying to counter such a swerve, the steering oar took control, kicked Mano in the stomach and catapulted him over the side in mountainous seas, whilst the boat drifted broadside and half swamped.

Mano tried to swim after the boat. The remaining youngsters did their best to slow down the drift with the oars, but broke and lost them. They threw out the sandbag anchor and attached sacks of green bananas to the line to slow down the drifting. Mano swam on but only sighted the boat in the distance when cresting a wave. The remaining boys cried and prayed for Mano. He was a very strong swimmer like his father (whose own adventures would fill another book).

Eventually, after many anxious hours, the weather abated. Mano made it back to the boat but was too weak to climb aboard without the help of the strongest to hoist him over the side where he wallowed in the bilge water in the bottom of the boat for a few hours to recover slowly.

Without any method of propulsion, they drifted for eight days almost without food. With cunning, they were able to spear the odd inquisitive fish that came too close to the drifting boat. They drank the blood of their catch and ate the flesh raw.

Using their hands and some floorboards, they paddled towards occasional rain clouds to collect water. One or two flying fish landed in the boat at night. Soon all the coconut water had been consumed and thirst started to take its toll. One of the two leaders, Steven, the only boy from Tongatapu, who later in life became an engineer, decided that they should distil fresh water from seawater by boiling it on the Primus stove and catching the runoff from the cooling vapour.

Sione lit the Primus and soon had some seawater on the boil. Unfortunately, the stove, balancing between his legs, upturned and burned his inner thigh. The wound later turned gangrenous and was agonizingly painful. As the lesion putrefied, the smell of rotting flesh made everybody nauseous. Later, however, some maggots hatched and miraculously ate out the putrefied flesh; and the wound healed itself after arrival on the island.

After eight days of hymn singing, praying, catching water in the rain showers, and becoming progressively weaker, the boys saw a dark rain cloud on the horizon. Next, they could discern seabirds flying in different directions in and out of the black cloud standing out like white flecks against a black background. All the boys knew that birds do not like flying in rain clouds and their hopes were raised. Finally, the cloud cleared revealing a high cliff-walled island, looking very small on the horizon to the north. They had no idea where they were, but they cheered weakly at the sight of land.

Although the boys did not know it, they must have already drifted southwards in a semi-circle past the island to be able to see it in the north. With fresh heart, they used the floorboards to paddle towards the land, with a little assistance from a southeast breeze. In their weakened state, their progress was slow. The wounded and smelly Sione lay half-conscious in the bottom of the boat.

By late afternoon on the next day, the would-be warriors were close to two large pinnacles of rock on the southwest corner of the island. The current pushed them off these cliffs and drove them northward up the west coast. They came close enough to drop the sand bag anchor, which held the boat outside the breakers and stopped the drifting.

Darkness fell and a meeting was held to choose someone to swim ashore in the dark, scout the layout and find a landing spot. The task fell to Mano who advised the boys, "If I don't come back, pull up the anchor and go because a wild animal might have eaten me—or worse!"

Mano dived over and, having torpedoed a few rocks in the surf with his head, he hit on the idea of clinging to seaweed roots on the outgoing surge and letting go to be thrown shoreward, battered and bruised, by the next incoming wave. It took a long time to land and he certainly did not feel like swimming back.

When he managed to get up on his feet, the whole island felt like it was moving. This was a new sensation for the boy, but a sensation experienced by many people after landing from a long voyage in a small boat. The noise of the surf was deafening. After resting, he yelled to the others that he had made it.

Mano as a 16-year-old

However, the boys mistook his yelling for instructions to beach the longboat. They were tired of waiting and very anxious to put their feet on land. In the dark, they paddled into the crashing breakers. The surf took over and hurtled the boat towards the rocks where it crashed and broke in two.

Hauling the wounded Sione through the waves, they staggered ashore amongst the volcanic rocks and boulders that had broken away from the sheer cliff faces along the stony coastline.

The so-called 'beach' on 'Ata Island

"I am here, I am here!" yelled Mano as he gathered up the boys. Before collapsing, they collected a few seabirds' eggs from nests close to the rocks, and downed the contents in a gulp. Some of the eggs had small, unhatched chicks in them. They spat out these feathery balls quickly.

Too exhausted to do anything else, they laid themselves down on higher ground and fell asleep whilst their boat pounded itself to pieces in the surf. Part of the gunwale that survived displayed Steven's carved notches for each day of the voyage; there were eight cuts on the board, and many more to come.

That was the end of a memorable voyage and the start of a long lonely stay on an unknown island where challenges would test their ingenuity and spiritual depth

Five of the six delinquents singing a hymn in the trees

Lonely life

I believe it was close to two years that the boys lived on the remote island of 'Ata before we found them. If they had been European lads, I do not think they would have survived.

Only with the practical down-to-earth survival instincts, such as these Tongan boys possessed, together with an early engagement with nature, and all this combined with spiritual strength, could any youngster have lived through such an ordeal.

In a later chapter about Middleton Reef, you will read about how four young shipwrecked Europeans, with different backgrounds and no common spiritual beliefs, found the challenges of life stranded on that reef insurmountable. It is my opinion that, if we had not turned up to rescue them, they would have been dead within a month.

Keeping a lookout for passing ships

Not so the Tongan boys! Their mode of life reflected a micro civilization where problems were solved and overcome. The two eldest were the leaders from the start, which is only natural in a tribal society.

When these two argued with one another, they may have been tempted to come to blows; but instead, they retreated from one another, and camped out and contemplated at opposite ends of the island until they had cooled down, by which time they may have figured out a compromising solution. Tensions in the group were eased by daily prayers and the singing of hymns.

For the first few months, the boys lived by the rocky seashore, sheltering from wind and rain beneath rock ledges. All were very weak after their eight-day drifting ordeal, and Sione lay suffering from his leg wound. When the healthiest one from among them saw some coconuts growing along the distant shore, he struggled over the rocks to gather some of the thirst-quenching nuts.

Fish were spiked with handmade spears and then eaten raw. Tame birds were snatched from their rookeries and strangled to provide blood, which was drained and drunk quickly. Seabird eggs were sucked dry.

As their strength improved, further exploration revealed an overgrown steep track leading towards the summit of the island 600 feet above. The boys made a slow ascent in stages clearing the track as they went.

On one ledge, the boys discovered a shallow grave with a skeleton and a large old knife blade. This became a very helpful tool in their survival kit. The skeleton was given a reburial service. Eventually they made it to the top of the island where an ancient volcanic crater revealed the home of previous inhabitants.

To their joy, wild taro, bananas, and other food plants had survived. Small bantam type Malaysian chickens were nesting in the trees and had been reproducing for over the 100 years since the last Tongans were evacuated by King Tupou I.

These welcome discoveries were seized upon by the enthusiastic and thankful boys. The crops were thinned and replanted in a crude way. The bantams were captured in improvised traps or run down by swift feet.

At last, Steven managed to light a fire by rubbing two dry sticks together. Once started, the fire was not allowed to go out. Each boy, in turn, was rostered to attend the fire day and night, and also to keep a lookout for passing ships. Some passing vessels were sighted but none saw the castaways.

A *fale* (grass hut) was erected and life became more restful as the boys shared the warmth of the hut with the fire and marauding rats. For sport, the boys made a badminton court with feathered shuttles.

One of the boys made a ukulele or small guitar from a plank and some rigging wire from the wrecked boat. Half coconuts lashed to the plank made up the sound chamber. I still have this instrument. Kolo composed seven songs whilst on the island.

As time passed, the homesick boys wondered if they would ever see their families again. To attract passing ships they had stock piled dried wood to light fires. On the night before we found them, they had lit one of their big bonfires to attract a large passenger ship, which passed by in the early evening.

One wonders if the cocktail-sipping passengers even noticed the distant fire. This must have been the fire that had caused the burned out patch on the green background, which I had spotted through the binoculars.

**An improvised shuttlecock game,
watched by a bantam hen, outside the rough shelter**

By the time we arrived, the boys were living as a small commune with a food garden, hollowed-out tree trunks to store rain water, a gymnasium with curious weights, a badminton court, chicken pens and a permanent fire, all resulting from their own skills and ingenuity—all this with only an old knife blade and much determination.

This was a picture of young resilience, a virtue or attribute that was to be demonstrated to me many times during my life amongst the Polynesian people. Many setbacks metamorphose into challenges to be overcome. Such lessons learnt often result in far-reaching benefits.

Sculpture by Fatai (Steven)
using the only piece of iron found on the island

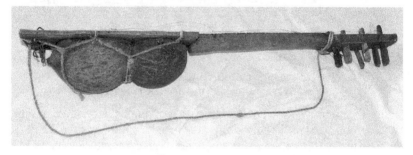

Guitar made from boat wreckage and two coconut shells

2. Eight days adrift and two years lost

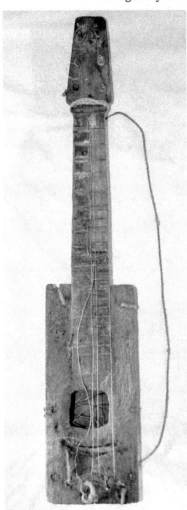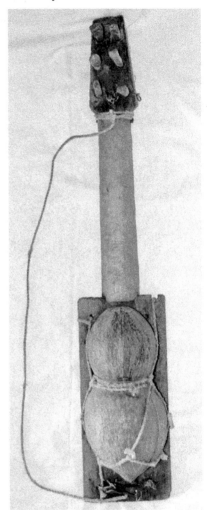

3
My first visit to Tonga

3
My first visit to Tonga

This first month of my 30 years in Tonga became a fast learning curve. Having arrived in Nuku'alofa on a winter day in 1966 on my 45-foot-long Tasmanian fishing boat *Just David* with the six, presumed dead, teenage survivors from the uninhabited island of 'Ata, we made fast to Vuna wharf. (Queen Sālote Wharf was under construction at the time.) We were boarded by some very overweight policemen who confiscated my guns and the six teenage criminals. The naughty boys were thrown into the strong wooden cells in the police station at the rear of the old customs house, and charged with not returning, and smashing the open sailing boat (*vakala*), which they had "borrowed" nearly two years previously.

Less than an hour later, a messenger from the English harbour master, Captain Chris Hill-Willis, delivered a note that said, "Get off my wharf"; so we moved to an anchorage off a stone jetty named the "yellow pier" and paddled ashore to investigate. A new hotel was under construction at the base of the wharf with the impressive name, "The International Dateline Hotel". It was financed by the British Government, which also financed the construction of Queen Sālote Wharf. I was later invited to attend the official opening of the Dateline and ordered a 'scotch on the rocks', which I shall always remember because the Tongan barman presented me with some coral rocks in the glass of scotch whiskey (instead of ice). Silly me!

As there were no banks in Tonga in 1966, I found myself at the Treasury (also housed in the customs house) investigating what local currency was available in exchange for American Express traveller's cheques. I was rewarded with a few Tongan ten-shilling notes and various coins. Tonga did not convert to the decimal currency of the Pa'anga until later and all sorts of foreign currency was circulating. The Treasurer, a New Zealand chap called Robbie Robertson, offered me a nice cup of tea and told me that his family managed the Government Guest House where I later stayed.

I found the owner of the *vakala* that the boys had "borrowed". He claimed his beautiful boat had been valued at £150. He stated that he was a generous and compassionate man, and would consider withdrawing his complaint and dropping the police charges against the boys if he could find this kind of money. Otherwise, the boys could learn their lesson in jail following the court case.

Six teenage 'criminals' outside their prison

Thinking that the saga of their survival would make an interesting TV documentary, I went to the local telegraph station and booked a shortwave radio phone call to the manager of Channel 7 in Sydney who was a mate of mine. He liked the idea of re-enacting the rescue and agreed to send a film crew on the next available flight. At that time there was only one return flight per week between Suva and the Fua'amotu grass airstrip. This was a DC3 carrying a few passengers, and a large life raft that occupied most of the cabin.

Meanwhile, the disheartened teenage prisoners in their khaki prison uniforms welcomed my visit to their dark remand cell, especially when I informed them that they would be released if they agreed to sail back to 'Ata on the FV *Just David* and re-enact their life as castaways on their 'desert island'. On the way, they could also visit their home island in the Ha'apai group where news of their rescue had spread. The families were gathering on the island of Ha'afeva to prepare a feast for the return of the prodigal sons, who had been given up as lost at sea.

Six-day welcome home party Ha'afeva Island in the Ha'apai group

A few days later, I met the DC3 on its arrival; and out stepped three film crew and one journalist. They were all pale-faced indoor studio types in their flared trousers and pointed city shoes. At this point, I did not ask them if they could swim through the surf at 'Ata and climb the 600 foot cliff to the boys' camp with all their camera gear. Instead, we water-sealed their equipment in plastic bags; and, having paid the *vakala* owner his £150, we 'sprung' the boys out of prison and sailed to Ha'apai with four very seasick camera crew passengers.

Landing on the beach at Ha'afeva, we were besieged by crying relatives. Some of these highly emotional reunion scenes were captured on camera as fathers and mothers greeted their lost sons.

Compassion and hospitality are Tongan virtues. The feasting, much kava drinking, dancing and praying lasted for six days. Each day, amongst many dishes, we ate crayfish. Crayfish hunting was the venture that had first lured me to Tonga; but, so far, I had had no success in finding any even with my up-to-date technology and

31

sophisticated equipment. Every day I asked to go catching crayfish with the fishermen. Every day they told me to wait for the party to finish before we started fishing.

Continuous Kava party, to celebrate boys' return home

Yet another turtle for the six day feast

Not having the patience of Tongans, I suggested we should at least prepare, find the bait and make ready any equipment that might be needed; but I was told to relax. On the sixth day, they asked me for a shilling to buy white gas for their pressure lantern; and we headed out on the reef at low tide after dark on what was a moonless night.

Siola'a reunited with his family

There, near the windward lip of the reef, crayfish had come out of the underwater caves and were crawling about in the shallow water in the darkness, easy to spear or pick up if one was quick. So much for western technology!

Usually there was one large bull crayfish amongst eight or nine smaller females, and I noticed in the lantern light that no one killed the big males but only took the females with or without eggs. This was a conservation practice, ensuring future reproduction by leaving the scarcer males. This practice was not followed on reefs far away from home where nobody cared about future catches.

Within half an hour, we had a sugar sack full of crays and headed for the shore. This experience gave me sufficient courage to plan a crayfish-gathering venture based in Tonga.

We then sailed off to the island of 'Ata with fond memories. The film crew gazed up at the stone face of 'Ata as we approached the steep island. The swell was breaking heavily even on the lee side of the island as the clouds of screaming seabirds zoomed overhead.

We launched the dinghy and, at this point, I asked the pale faces if they could surf and swim through the breakers to the black beach with its loosely rumbling stones surging back and forth with the waves. None claimed to be swimmers of any sort but I assured them that the Tongan teenagers would help them make the shore. All Ha'apai kids can usually swim before they can walk.

We bundled the film crew into the dinghy, rowed them to the lip of the first breakers and dumped them overboard. Through the crystal-clear water, we could see them heading downwards towards the bottom. Like trained lifesavers, the boys dove down, brought them to the surface and pushed them through the surf to torpedo their heads into the perilous rocks.

The film crew flopped on the rocky shore, spluttering and spent, whilst we landed the wrapped camera gear by forming a line of the boys in the surf and throwing the equipment from one to another. Then I explained to the camera crew that they now had a long clamber along the rocky shore to the base of the track leading steeply to the boys' camp 600 feet up the cliff-face.

Needless to say, the Sydney city crew were exhausted and grazed by the time they made it to the rat-infested camp. They could do little filming that day and evening, but managed to catch a few hours of disturbed sleep on the hard earthen floor of the unstable *fale* that the boys had built a year earlier.

After a poor sleep, the still exhausted crew started rolling some black and white 16-mm film, only sufficient to edit into a half-hour documentary. The filming quality was generally poor. After we departed in the FV *Just David*, they remembered that they had left some exposed rolls of film somewhere on the island. Consequently, most of the edited film was disappointing; but the story remained exciting.

After returning to Nukuʻalofa and dispatching the film crew, I was surprised to be summonsed to an audience with the new king, Tupou IV. His mother, Queen Sālote, had died only about a half a year earlier and the country was still mourning before his coronation.

With my friend and crewmember, Peter Currie, we arrived at His Majesty's summer retreat to be greeted by one of the largest men I had ever seen.

The King (left) and I (right)

In his early 40s, Tupou IV stood over 6-foot tall and, at the time, weighed about 28 stone (390 lb or 178 kg). My hand disappeared into his—which resembled the huge flipper of a seal—to be crushed with a friendly handshake. Later in life, he lost some weight, and exercised by wearing a lead-weighted vest and climbing up and down the Palace stairway.

His Majesty graciously thanked me for rescuing six of his young delinquent subjects, and asked if there was anything Tonga could do for us as a token of his appreciation. It sprang to my mind that approval would be needed if I should return with my family and boats to start commercial fishing for crayfish and anything else that swims. His

Majesty agreed to my request for approval to fish and said we would be welcome.

We fuelled up the *Just David*, said a temporary goodbye to new friends and the six delinquents, and departed for Australia, not to return for two years.

4
Preparations back in Australia

4
Preparations back in Australia

On returning home to Sydney after my first visit and voyage to Tonga in 1967, a big decision had to be made. I wanted to drag my wife and kids to a new life in Tonga. Why? Life was good in Australia and the family were happy in Sydney—but I was not.

Apart from the lure of lucrative crayfish catching, there were other reasons to leave Australia and move to the Kingdom of Tonga. Justine and I had just finished a four-year legal battle with the Australian Tax Office to recover a large amount of money from an incorrect assessment and an unjustified fine imposed upon us by the Australian Government. Under draconian Australian tax laws, one is automatically declared guilty until one proves oneself innocent. After those four years of frustration and heavy legal expenses, we eventually recovered all our money. However, the experience left us with a feeling of injustice in the system; and I was looking for some country, which followed British traditional legal justice of presumed innocence until proven guilty.

I had discovered that Tonga used British common law plus a few local statutes. At the time, the Tongan statutes filled only one book of law, instead of the large number of law books found in other "advanced" societies. My father had always taught me that every written law made by man is negative, in as much as they all state: "Thou SHALT NOT do this or that"; and if you do, the penalty shall be such and such. It follows, then, that the country with the fewest laws must be inhabited by the freest people.

To illustrate this point, even back in the 1950s, I remember a dear friend and Tasmanian commercial fisherman, Roy Downey, had painted on the outside of his boat's wheelhouse a long list of legal requirements, which included:

- Boat name and registered Commonwealth fishing licence number
- Master fisherman's licence number
- Tasmanian fishing boat licence number

- Crayfish limited trap (pot) licence number
- Long line permit number
- Radio operator's licence number
- Driver's licence number
- Dog licence number
- Gun and harpoon licence number
- Marriage licence number

Beneath this, he had written in large letters "GOD SAVE THE FREE BRITISH SUBJECT". Unfortunately, he was lost with his crew when his vessel struck a cliff in southwest Tasmania.

With the idea of freedom in my head, a freedom from union blackmailing, bureaucratic inflexibility, and all people and laws telling you what not to do, I thought Tonga looked promising. At this stage, I did not appreciate that cultural customs and traditions under the feudal-type pecking order in Tonga often overrode British common law and even sometimes the local statutes.

So, with adventure in my heart, I planned to up anchor and prepare for a new life with the family. Warwick Hood, my naval architect friend, was commissioned to design the 70-foot MV *Ata*, which was to be a refrigerated, steel fishing vessel to act as mothership for the crayfish hunting.

MV *Ata* under construction

Fitted with an 8-cylinder Gardner diesel of 200-horse power, MV *Ata* was built in 1967 at Stannard Bros shipyard in North Sydney. The ship was later stretched or jumboized to 80-foot. Apart from referring to the memorable deserted island, the name of MV *Ata* also had the benefit of being short, starting with an "A" and spelling the same way backwards.

MV *Ata*'s launch day

It joined the Tongan registry under the official number 76. Not many ships registered in Tonga in those days. A new crew would be needed for the new vessel, so I decided to sponsor the six rescued delinquents for a visit to Sydney to train in various seafaring skills and also to learn "hooker" diving equipment, which we planned to use when reef fishing. During their stay in Sydney, the boys camped in the rumpus room of our suburban house.

Fatai went off daily to a diesel workshop and Mano learned European cooking from my wife. The rest of us went to the shipyard to help and learn, except on the weekends when it was time for some teenage mischief instead.

Preparing MV *Ata* for sea trials

It was to take two years of preparation before the family and I departed Sydney for Nuku'alofa. As our departure date neared, Mano developed elephantiasis or filariasis, a common disease in Polynesia but rare in Australia. He was hospitalized and his scrotum shaved so that many young Australian trainee doctors and medical students could file through his ward to inspect and study this rare swelling. Unnerved by this scrutiny and fearful that he might lose his manhood, Mano escaped from the hospital one night and made his way several kilometres to our house in his hospital gown. He refused to return to the hospital until I promised him that no knife would be used other than to take a sample for a biopsy. He was eventually cured by drugs.

However, he was too sick to sail with us to Auckland, so we sailed with no trainee cook. He remained with Justine for further cooking lessons until well enough to join us in New Zealand.

MV *Ata* sea trials

Meanwhile, I had sold two of my Tasmanian fishing boats with their licences but kept the well-travelled FV *Just David*. I resigned my many clubs and professional associations. We rented out the house and mothballed the car. Justine and the kids prepared to fly to Tonga after I had arrived there and found suitable accommodation.

5
New home and work in Tonga

5
New home and work in Tonga

Justine and the kids had been none too keen about moving to a remote Pacific island, and leaving all their friends and comfortable Sydney lifestyle. So I had to make their new life here as reasonably comfortable as possible.

When Justine and the three children arrived in Nuku'alofa, Tonga, in 1968, our first home was the house of Tofa Ramsay in Railway Rd, opposite the old telephone exchange. Before connecting any phone calls, the telephone operators could tell callers whether we were at home or not just by looking out of their window. This spying and messaging system worked well. Although our address was Railway Rd, there was no longer any railway in Tonga. Around the turn of the century, there had been a railway that carried copra from the lagoon to Nuku'alofa's wharf.

Nuku'alofa's electricity was supplied from an old slow-revving diesel generator located a few streets away. Lying in bed on her first night in Tonga, Justine said, "That train has been a long time at the station. I can still hear its motor running." Of course, it was no train but only the generator, which never stopped running.

Like myself, Tofa was a boat owner. He and his wife operated some small diesel-powered wooden vessels around Tonga, carrying cargo and passengers. We shared the house and telephone with their family and extended family. The young children of both families played together. Our two girls attended the Side School, being the only English speaking primary school at that time.

Before long, we were able to lease a large old wooden villa on the waterfront three doors from the Palace, and next to the British High Commission. Known as Nukasa (Newcastle), it had been the house of the old noble 'Ulukālala, whose widow had moved to the residence of her young relative, the Baron Vaea.

With the creaking old wooden house came the old retinue including a small black Solomon Islander named Malala (coal) who had been his

47

late master's mascot. In those days and earlier it was fashionable for chiefs to keep a foreign native or two as mascots for good luck. Also with the house came the ghosts. My imaginative children claimed they saw a pair of black shiny shoes wandering through the house on some nights. His widow confirmed that 'Ulukālala did have a pair of polished pointy black shoes. Our cook was the gigantic Sele who produced wonderful Tongan and European dishes on the old wood-fired stove. Justine grew to hate the stove and oven in the tropical heat. We remember my hardworking wife cooking Christmas feasts on this stove, dripping perspiration and then needing to have a cold shower before sitting down at the table.

Vuna Wharf 1968

Young Peter Junior, at 3 or 4 years, swam in the lagoon out front at high tide on the reef. His was the only white bottom amongst all the brown bottoms splashing about. He could nearly swim before he could walk. One day he escaped the watchful eye of the house girl and dodged past the Palace guards, to arrive running onto the Palace veranda.

The very tall Queen Mata'aho stepped out and looked down on this small pale kid and asked, "Who are you?" She recalls that he looked up and said impudently, "I am Peter Warner, who are you?" to which Mata'aho said, "I am the Queen." Recently I had been teaching the children not to believe everything that Tongans told them; so little

Peter looked up to the Queen and then asked, "True or lie?" Meanwhile our house girl hastily put on her plaited mat (*ta'ovala*) and raced to the Palace to retrieve the little miscreant. Her Majesty had a good laugh and retold the story many times.

Justine and our local noble, Hon Fakafanua, 1968

As there were no banks in Tonga, one of my first business acts was to open a trader's account at the treasury as the equivalent of a bank account. After a nice chat and cup of tea with the treasurer, Robbie Robertson, he declared the Tongan currency (Pa'anga) account open, and converted and deposited a traveller's cheque.

I asked how I could withdraw money or pay accounts from it. Did they issue chequebooks? No, but he told me that I could send someone in with a signed slip of paper to withdraw cash. I asked if he would recognize my signature to which he said, "In time." I then asked if the trader's account earned interest to which he said, "No luck." Naively, I asked if the treasury had any loan facilities. He patiently explained that the government did not lend money.

Without banks, it was customary for Tongan traders to keep large steel safes, and act as custodians of other people's cash, especially as most locals did not trust the Government treasury. I remember Tofa leaving his savings with the Riechelmann Bros for safekeeping until he wanted to buy a new motor or another boat.

Our house, Nukasa, was also our office and was equipped with a safe. Justine had the key and, whenever I was away, acted as chief cashier. The first Tongan crew member whom I sacked was dismissed with a note from me, telling Justine to pay him his outstanding wages. This cunning young single man found a young girl in rags whom he claimed as his wife and arrived at Nukasa with an infant painted with iodine who was supposedly sick.

Through tearful eyes and with a gift of tapa cloth for my wife, they then put on an act of despair asking how they could afford medicine and Glaxo for their sick child after I had sacked its father. Justine was very sympathetic and generous to them. When I arrived home, Justine accused me of being a mean, hard and unsympathetic boss, until I explained their impudent deception to squeeze as much money as possible from her.

Another disturbing experience at Nukasa happened one night when a disturbed youth removed outside window louvres leading to the girls' bedroom. He climbed in and Carolyn was woken by the lad in bed with her. She let out a loud scream and kneed him in the groin. By the time I arrived on the scene, the lad had disappeared through the window with me in full pursuit. Luckily, he got away because I might have killed him.

Nonetheless, we all enjoyed living at Nukasa. I was away a lot, skippering the boats and managing the fishing operations. We started hunting crayfish in the Ha'apai group of islands. On top and on the windward sides of the many reefs, the crayfish dwelt in small coral caves. They would not enter traps or pots in any number and we soon gave up scuba diving because of coral damage to diving equipment and wet suits.

Whilst it was my plan just to hunt crayfish, the divers speared every moving thing around them from fish to turtles. All this was cleaned and went into the freezer. Fish, stingrays, sharks, octopus, clams, sea urchins and other delicacies were brought back to the capital of Nuku'alofa where crowds gathered around the wharf eager to buy all this cheap protein. Live but wounded turtles were kept upside down on deck much to my family's horror. The plan to catch crayfish and export crayfish tails quickly broadened into fishing and selling everything else to the locals.

Whenever there was an immediate need for cash, all the fishermen were active. This only occurred when school fees were required or when the churches called for donations (*misinale*). In between, we often waited, with freezer running, for the fishermen and divers to show up. They often had more important things to do such as playing the guitar, kava club gatherings, weddings and funerals or weeding their vegetable gardens.

Patience is not one of my virtues. Some of the older men went fishing at night in their outrigger canoes and returned at dawn with their fish. Hand line fishing always requires patience, a virtue that the Tongans possess in plenty. To sit in an outrigger from sunset to dawn on a dark night, entertained only by flashes of deep phosphorescent activity, gives one time to think and practice self-discipline whilst exploring the stars.

The land-based ladies hunted the reefs for shellfish and octopus. These wise people did not want paper money for their catch. Paper money only got wet when you went swimming and it could not be eaten. It was utterly useless. What they wanted in exchange for their catch was sugar, or flour, or biscuits or canned corn beef—not paper printed by untrustworthy governments or banks. Ingots or coins made of silver were slightly more acceptable. These untutored economists made a lot of sense.

I quickly got the message; and it was not long before I had a small lockable store on board MV Ata—and, later, ashore—full of foreign "poisonous" luxuries like corned beef, sugar and tobacco to damage their health in exchange for their nourishing fish.

This system of exchange went on for many years. I recall one old weather-beaten fisherman, complaining one day that my clerk had cheated him by supplying a smaller quantity of raw sugar than he had received previously for the same quantity and size of fish. I tried to explain to him that the price of Fiji sugar had increased and therefore we could not give him the same quantity as before.

51

The old man took me to the weighing scales where his fish were hanging and asked me if that was the same number of fish and size that he always had presented. I had to say, "Yes." He then took me to the sack of sugar and looked inside. He asked if that was the same sugar that he had always received in the past; and, again, I had to say, "Yes." He then demanded the same quantity of sugar for the same fish as previously. He would not listen to my explanation in my poor and stumbling Tongan. He did not want to hear about inflation, price rises measured in paper money or such strange things as exchange rates. All he wanted was the same sugar for the same fish. It was a good exercise in uncomplicated economics. One could not argue against his logical point, so I gave him more sugar. Later I solved the problem for myself by increasing the selling price of the fish to the public in Nuku'alofa.

Spearing under the breakers was one of the daylight methods of fishing because most sea creatures enjoy energized waters. One had to be quick and try to spear the crayfish in the body because we wanted the tail undamaged for export. Of course, one could not easily see if it was male or female in the rush and many were egg-carrying females. As it was a bit late to throw them back when dead, we took them all.

Another method was looking for the small coral caves or holes on top of the reef at low water. Usually one could see the feelers of the bull crayfish guarding the entrance to the hole. If speared or grabbed, the eight or more females, hiding behind the bull, would scatter, but if one felt behind the bull, one could extract the females first and leave the bull until last.

What we had come to catch

Using this method, the locals never went back to the same reef more than once per year so that a new crayfish family could have time to take up residence in the old hole. This natural conservation method was in practice long before foreign advisors and experts arrived.

Of course, away from the home reefs, the fishermen created havoc, smashing up coral holes with crow bars to extract the crayfish. Everything that moved on the reef was taken, from giant clams and other shellfish to every variety of fish or turtle. This was all carried to the MV *Ata* for weighing, processing and freezing.

We would anchor the mother ship in the lee of reefs or in lagoons as near to a village as possible. The crayfish were bought from the divers for export and other seafood was bought from men, women and children in Ha'apai for resale in Nuku'alofa.

During one long fishing voyage around Ha'apai, we anchored up for Sunday in the lee of Mango Island. Whilst the crew were ashore at church, I kept anchor watch on this calm morning. Through my binoculars, I followed the movements of an old lady outside her hut on the foreshore and noticed many chickens pecking around her yard. Where there are chickens, there must be eggs, thought I, and I have not eaten an egg for a few weeks. So I paddled ashore in a canoe and asked the old lady in my dreadful Tongan, whether I could buy some eggs.

"What do you want eggs for?" she asked.

"So I can cook and eat them" I replied.

"Stupid foreigner! Why don't you be patient and wait for the egg to become a chicken and then eat the bird?" she explained in an exasperated tone.

However, the old lady finally agreed to my unusual request so I asked, "Where are the eggs?" She pointed to the bush surrounding the hut and explained to this stupid foreigner, "Go and find the nests!"

Apart from acting as cashier and banker whenever I was away from home, Justine also had to attend to all the new domestic situations. This included guarding our own refrigerated stores, such as the butter, which had a habit of disappearing from our refrigerator in the kitchen.

Young Peter enjoyed life to the fullest with his newfound friends. He quickly learned to talk and swear beautifully in Tongan. The two girls did well at the Side School, which had a good New Zealand principal, Mr Clarke. Gradually the family started to enjoy and appreciate life in the Kingdom.

So that the fishing business in Ha'apai could continue while the mother ship MV *Ata* was away delivering crayfish tails and refuelling in Fiji, I decided to build some barges with freezer capacity to anchor in Ha'apai and later also in Vavau. These were made of Ferro cement and plastered upside down on the beach at Touliki where I had leased some land from the Honourable Fakafonua. With the help of a New Zealand boat builder, we trained up a local team of Ferro cement plasterers who became quite skilled.

Coconut logs were used to slide the upside-down barges into the sea. 50 or 60 strong men on the end of ropes heaved the load out onto the reef at high tide. The air pocket within the inverted barge kept it afloat until we reached deeper water beyond the reef. Then we tipped the barge over and sank it to sit upright on a sandy bottom. Divers tied upturned steel drums to the barge and then pumped air into the drums. With the drums acting like underwater balloons, the barges floated to the surface and were bailed out.

When the barges were completed, the New Zealand builder went home, leaving me with a skilled team with nothing to do. So I had the stupid idea that we could build island-style round houses cheaply in Ferro cement. The half-an-egg shaped roof dome was formed over a mould on the ground and then jacked up to two metres and supported on posts. They were available with or without walls. Ferro cement is made from a thin layer of cement over fine wire netting. The domes were very strong from the outside but they were easily punctured from the inside—just like an egg is; otherwise, a chick could not punch its way out of its shell.

The idea was to build the domes at home and transport them to their destination on the back of a truck. This limited the diameter of the house to the width of Tongan roads, hence the houses were quite small, only about four metres wide. To demonstrate them we built three in a triangle at Touliki and moved into them from our Nukasa villa. Then I waited for the flood of orders from the Tongan community for cheap houses in the old island style, but with the advantage of being hurricane and earthquake proof. A few foreigners bought them and imagined they were romantically living in an island-style house but the locals shunned them. Tongans wanted to show off in European-style square boxes.

In our three Ferro cement houses close to the beach, I had explained to Justine and the kids that they had nothing to fear as the houses were earthquake proof because of the flexibility of the Ferro cement. However, earthquakes are often followed by tidal waves (tsunamis).

Therefore, if there was to be an earthquake whilst I was away, they were to hang onto their mattresses when the sea came in the windows, and float up to the ceiling where they would be held in an air pocket inside the dome. Their ears might pop with the pressure but they would safely float down when the tidal wave retreated.

In 1976, there was a 7.5 Richter scale earthquake whilst I was at sea near Vavau and I felt nothing. However, the family experienced its full effect, which lasted about eight minutes in all. It started off as a slow waltz, then a foxtrot and finally a rock and roll. In Tongan tradition, some locals were already out banging tins and steel drums to awaken Maui who was supposed to hold up Tonga, but who had obviously dozed off. Of course, the power was out, but the family held onto their mattresses waiting for the tidal wave that never came. The aftermath revealed that many statues and bells fell off churches, which also cracked in places. The ministers of religion could not explain why the churches suffered damage but all the hotels and drinking establishments survived unscathed.

The Ferro cement round house sales dried up so I had to come up with another product to keep the trained team and cement mixers busy. The quality of water was always substandard in Tonga and we know clean water helps reduce illnesses, so it was easy to figure out that affordable Ferro cement tanks would be a winner because they would be cheap and easily transported to place under house roofs. Ours were 8 feet in diameter and 8 feet high, moulded on a concrete base with steel lifting eyes. We made, sold and delivered more than 100 in Tongatapu, Ha'apai and Vavau before I left Tonga, and the design has been adopted by many. This demonstrates that simple solutions are always the best.

I had come to Tonga to catch and export crayfish tails to luxury markets but in the process became involved in killing any fish life with which to supplement the diet of a protein-deficient people. Having enlarged the fishing endeavour to the maximum using local fishermen, I soon observed that my feeble attempts to flood the Tongan market with cheap fish would never be achieved. Another source of cheap and tasty protein had to be found.

Some say Tongans live in a well-fed poverty and there is always something to eat, such as fruit and root crops; but that is not protein. Feeding people has always been a subject near to my heart, especially following an early teenage seaman's experience. In Shanghai in the winter of 1949, tip-truckloads of the corpses of starved residents were were tipped into the Whangpoa creek fore and aft of the moored ship.

Mao and his army had surrounded and starved the city occupied by Government troops. The scene still haunts me; and I admire the many methods used today by the Chinese Government to secure food for its people.

To be of some better service to the Tongan population, I hit upon the idea of carrying Tongan bananas to New Zealand and returning to Tonga with frozen lamb flaps, which were cheap, greasy and a very popular protein source. That became the start of Warner Pacific Line, the story of which belongs in another chapter.

6
Minerva Reef

6
Minerva Reef

Returning to reef fishing—among our best-yielding hunting grounds were two coral atolls that lay awash 200 miles south of Tongatapu. Originally known as North Minerva Reef and South Minerva Reef, they were renamed in 1972 by His Majesty Tupou IV as Teleki Tokelau and Teleki Tonga. Brett's South Pacific Pilot book published in 1887–8 states their accurate position was established by Captain Denham RN in the HMS *Herald* in 1851.

Each of these two atolls has a navigable entrance on the western side about a cable wide and 15 fathoms deep, which leads into a round lagoon over three miles in diameter. The lagoons are brilliant crystal-clear gems in a still and reflecting calm except at high tide when the windward surf breaks over the atoll rim and disturbs the mirror-like calm of the anchorages.

Except for the numerous nigger heads of coral, the bottoms of the lagoons are covered with a layer of sand about six inches thick over a base of smooth coral rock. This does not make for a secure anchorage to grip onto, but heavy anchors and heavy chain resist the tendency to drag ground tackle except in severe hurricane conditions.

The surf breaking on the windward side is visible in daylight from a small vessel about three or four miles away in clear conditions, but not so at night in calm conditions or in daylight in rainy weather. Consequently, the reefs are littered with old and new wrecks. For those who have it, radar is useful. Captain Tevita (David) Fifita, who wrecked one of Tofa Ramsay's boats—the *Tuaikaepau*—on the reef, said his helmsman did not see it on a calm night as he was steering into the moon's reflective path.

Tevita Fifita became famous in 1962 when he and most of his crew survived on the reef on an abandoned Japanese wreck for many weeks. Finally, he made a raft out of the debris and sailed to Fiji in a starving condition to alert the authorities who recovered the surviving Tongan crewmembers from Minerva Reef after more than 100 days of endurance. Of course, one does not go hungry there. There is so much delicious seafood to collect as well as green seaweed and moss for vitamins. However, drinking water is a problem unless you can distil seawater. Carbohydrates are scarce so one loses weight quickly.

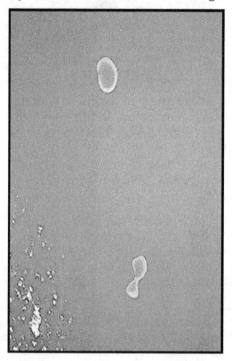

North and South Minerva Reefs from above

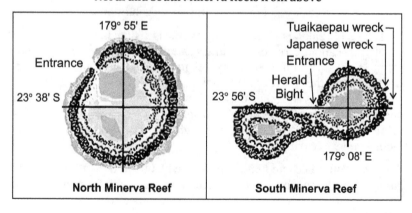

North Minerva Reef:
179° 55' E
Entrance
23° 38' S
North Minerva Reef

South Minerva Reef:
Tuaikaepau wreck
Japanese wreck
Entrance
Herald Bight
23° 56' S
179° 08' E
South Minerva Reef

6. Minerva Reef

Survivors of the *Tuaikaepau*, 1962[1]

Japanese wreck on Minerva Reef

---

[1] See: Olaf Ruhen, *Minerva Reef.* Minerva Bookshop, Auckland, 1963.

After anchoring inside the lagoon close up to the windward lip of the reef, our method of operation was to launch our two workboats and all the outriggers we carried on deck. Up to 20 skilled divers from Ha'apai would head for the windward reef and take anything that moved, but in particular speared the crayfish, which were plentiful then. Towards sunset, they would return to MV *Ata* where the whole crew of nine would start weighing, processing and freezing the catch. This took a large portion of the night, while the fishermen slept in any unoccupied corner of the ship and under a tarpaulin on deck. It was a crowded ship but I had inflatable life rafts and vests for 40 people.

During the day, when the fishermen were away, I spent time exploring the windward rim of the reef and diving in the surge channels. At low tide, one could walk along the top of the reef rim, which was roughly the width of a two-lane country road full of pot holes, cracks and crevices. In fact, one could have driven a four-wheel-drive car along it.

The constant wave action kept the rim cleared and maintained a level surface except in crevices where one found all sorts of delicious morsels, particularly shellfish and sea urchins. Diving and snorkelling amongst the colourful life was a wonderful experience in this tropical undersea world of spectacular beauty, leading one to ponder on other worlds unknown to us.

My main objective was to look for wreckage and debris of old ships that had met their end here. Clues were everywhere. An old ship's anchor embedded on top of the windward reef indicated that a desperate captain had tried to stop drifting onto the reef, but current and waves had won the battle. Pieces of iron ballast wedged in crevices were all that was left of a wooden ship that had been ripped open and pounded to pieces. On the bottom of the lagoon inside the windward rim were remnants of old iron fastenings and rigging gear encrusted with coral.

One day whilst diving, I found the remains of the ivory keyboard of a piano, which started me thinking that only big wooden passenger ships carried pianos for high-paying passengers, and that the piano had probably been housed in the saloon near the Captain's quarters. Sailing ship captains of large vessels kept a safe in their cabins for the valuables of passengers and officers. So I thought there must be a safe close to the remains of the ivory keyboard.

Next day I halted fishing operations, and everybody started looking underwater for a safe and other valuable items. I thought we might become rich if the contents of the safe could be recovered. It did not take long for the divers to discover the safe but it was open and empty except for sand and coral. We returned to fishing and I lost interest in wrecks. However, one cannot but wonder how many lives were lost on these early uncharted reefs, lonesome in the middle of the Pacific on a sailing ship route from North America towards Australia and New Caledonia. Not only myself but also other members of our group, both Europeans and Tongan, felt an unexplainable sense of attachment to unknown beings, as if wandering spirits were still hanging around the reefs wanting to communicate. This phenomenon has visited me in other remote places but never as strongly as that on Minerva Reef.

We experienced a near disaster at South Minerva in February 1970. I had appointed a very competent Tongan Captain, Uiki Ofa, to command the MV *Ata* whilst I attended to other matters. Uiki with our crew and a team of Ha'apai fishermen with outrigger canoes were operating during the hurricane season but it was rare that hurricanes reached as far south as Minerva Reef.

In case of bad weather arising during fishing operations, my standing orders were to gather all the boats and canoes on board as soon as possible and head out through the pass before the exit became a raging surge of breaking waves as the storm overfilled the lagoon with huge rolling breakers. In a storm, it is impossible to distinguish the exit passage amidst the turmoil of breaking seas. Of course, if one can make it out to the ocean, it is possible to manoeuver away from the center of a storm.

Late one morning, Uiki realized that a storm or hurricane was approaching and signalled for the boats to return. Some had wandered too far away to hear the ship's horn or see the signal flags. After a lengthy recovery involving sending a workboat to rescue some canoes, all were safely aboard, but by this time, it was too late and too dangerous to steam out of the lagoon. Uiki anchored the vessel as best he could be using two anchors and all the chain we had. The wind was now so strong from the west that the anchors started to drag, so he started the main engine to steam ahead to ease the strain on the anchors and stop the drift. All his efforts could not stop the full strength hurricane from throwing the ship up onto the lip of the reef.

The hurricane pounded and propelled the steel hull across the top of the reef towards the nearby ocean. At this time some of the fishermen panicked and wanted to launch and get into the inflatable life rafts, which would have been lost if they had succeeded. Uiki pointed my rifle at them and threatened to shoot them if they did not stop their attempt. This worked; otherwise, they would have disappeared into the foaming seas never to be seen again.

Meanwhile the anchors had gripped the inside or lagoon side of the reef's rim, stopping the passage of the damaged ship all the way across the top and into the ocean. Then in the murky grey-green darkness came the calm as the eye of the hurricane passed overhead. Shortly, the wind reversed and blew from the east, blowing and dragging the ship back across the top of the rim of the reef towards the lagoon, where it finally became wedged in a surge channel close to the edge of the water. Fortunately, it was not blown right back into the lagoon because it would have sunk, having developed numerous holes and splits in the steel hull. The storm passed and power was restored with the generators.

Uiki radioed his situation to me in Nuku'alofa. Fortunately, the *Just David* was in port, and I hurriedly put together a salvage plan. I borrowed some dynamite from the Public Works Department (PWD), and a portable welder and underwater welding rods. We also loaded empty watertight drums and diving gear. We set out and found the dinted and listing MV *Ata* perched on top of the reef where the crew were more than happy to see us.

The fishermen from Ha'apai had been rescued by the Tongan Government oceangoing tug *Hifofua* and taken home. Whilst the crew dug and blew an escape channel through the coral into the lagoon, we welded up some cracks and holes at low water. Then, with sledgehammers, we partially straightened out some of the bends in two propeller blades. Finally, we strapped empty drums under the hull at low water and waited for the tide to rise and refloat the ship, which came out through the excavated coral channel with the help of *Just David* acting as a tug. The drums were removed and the stinking fish were thrown overboard from the flooded freezer. The pumps all worked and the main engine was started. At slow ahead we all returned to Nuku'alofa.

Although these two remote reefs were 200 miles south of Tongatapu, and technically in international waters, Tonga had always regarded them as her own, even though they were totally submerged at high tide. Sometime in about 1971, some enterprising Americans tried to create an entity called "The Republic of Minerva", and announced they were going to anchor a mother ship in the lagoon and claim the reefs as a tax-free haven with a floating bank and pirate radio station. The ship would be the capital of the new republic and the lagoons would become the claimed territory of the Republic.

Minervan $35 coin

This caused some concern to His Majesty Tupou IV who took costly international legal advice on the situation to learn, firstly, that only recognised countries, not random groups of people or companies, could claim lands or territories; and, secondly, Minerva Reefs were not claimable by anyone because they were not land. Land must be above high water mark to be defined as land. Thirdly, a country's claim to new land or territory must be recognised by some if not all the governments of nearby neighbouring countries.

His Majesty, therefore, asked the diplomats of Australia, New Zealand and France if they would recognise Tonga's old claim to the reefs if he built some artificial islands on the reefs, all above high water mark. I do not think he asked the Fiji Government who still dispute Tonga's claim to the two reefs. Following the provisional diplomatic approval of the idea by the major neighbouring countries, His Majesty ordered the building of two artificial islands in early 1971—and who do you think became involved?

By this time, I had expanded the fishing fleet to a small flotilla of boats to fish and act as dormitories for the fishermen. They included the 40-foot fiberglass freezer boat *Otu Motu Lalo* and a 28-foot launch *Hala Toa Ongo* as well as the *Just David*. Sometimes, escorted by the MV *Ata*, we would all sail in convoy to Minerva Reef to continue our pillage of the underwater life.

The Tongan Department of Public Works was in charge of the artificial island construction. The Department chartered two of my boats to transport materials and labour to the site. The director also consulted me on many matters concerning the construction and siting of the islands. Besides dynamite, crowbars and underwater cement, we emptied the jail of a large contingent of prisoners to manually excavate and lift the coral rocks into position.

During the operation, one prisoner argued with another and, in the heated dispute, one was speared with a crow bar, through the chest by another. The prisoner died instantly. The one and only prison warden in charge said we should freeze the body in the fish hold of the MV *Ata* and chain the murderer to the mast before sailing back to Nuku'alofa as soon as possible, leaving the remaining prisoners to get on with the job.

My superstitious crew were not very happy to have the body in the fish freezer hold but we did not tell the public who bought the fish in Nuku'alofa that their fish dinner had shared space with a corpse.

After this unfortunate incident, the construction of the two islands was completed, one over the grave of a shipwrecked Japanese long liner. The finished top of the islands only measured 20 feet by 20 feet with sloping shoulders of rocks into the sea. A flagpole was erected on each before the King arrived on the Government ferry with entourage for the flag raising ceremony.

On each of these tiny islets the pantomime-like protocol was performed. First, the magnificently uniformed police band assembled, and then a polished army company prepared for the 21-gun salute. All the ministers of the crown and the ministers of the leading churches crammed onto the small space on a sweltering hot calm day. His Majesty came ashore with his immediate minders. We commoners crowded the sloping rock foundations.

The police band played the national anthem, and then many ministers of the church intoned long prayers. Finally, the Prime Minister read out the proclamation formally annexing the islands as part of The Kingdom of Tonga.

The flag was raised as the 21-gun salute was fired into the middle of the still quiet ocean, and the band played the Tongan national anthem to us and the seabirds on these two specks in the vast Pacific Ocean.

Then we paddled back to the Government ferry where all enjoyed a huge feast of fish, giant clams and turtle supplied by our crew. If Gilbert and Sullivan had lived in this period, they could have composed a delightful comic opera of this performance.

Sometime after I left Tonga, the Government erected a beacon on Teleki Tonga—a Fijian gunboat shot up and destroyed it in 2010. The Junta that ruled Fiji at the time were annoyed with a successful exercise executed by the Tongan Navy to extract a senior Fijian officer with Tongan connections, thought to be a dissenter, from under their noses. A Tongan patrol boat cruised into the Fijian coast one dark night and rescued the officer without the knowledge of the Fijians. The Fijian Junta were not pleased that a Tongan vessel had sneaked, undetected, into their unwatched coastline. The Tongans replaced the beacon on Minerva in 2011.

7
Middleton Reef

7
Middleton Reef

MV *Ata* had been built 60 foot in length in 1968 and nearly wrecked on Minerva Reef in 1970, undergoing repairs to her damaged hull and propeller in Fiji. With time, I conceived a notion that if the MV *Ata* could be elongated to 80 foot, it would not only add to her capacity, but her resulting sleek profile would increase her speed without the need for any additional power.

So, in 1972, we sailed from Tonga back to the Richmond River in Australia, stopping briefly at Middleton Reef on the way to catch a few fish. Middleton Reef is a rich source of marine life and only about 200 miles east of the Richmond River.

Like other estuarine rivers in the northern regions of NSW, the Richmond River had been the home of small ship and fishing boat builders; but, by 1972, the industry was in decline and the surviving builders were looking for work.

York Bros at Swan Bay on the Richmond River won the job of Jumbo-sizing the MV *Ata*. She was cut in two, and I and the Tongan crew witnessed her two halves being winched apart. When the Tongans saw the huge gap, they despaired of my silly idea and thought they would never see Tonga again. However, the addition of the extra 20 foot of hull went well; and with her total length of 80 foot, the MV *Ata* hull speed improved and the freezer size was doubled.

The York Brothers had done such a good job in extending the MV *Ata*'s overall length that I decided to return to their shipyard in 1974 for her annual survey and maintenance repairs as well as to fit some new deep-sea fishing equipment.

In June, after MV *Ata*'s overhaul was completed we underwent trials of the new equipment with Bill York, the shipyard co-owner, on-board. We ran into bad weather outside the continental shelf east of the Richmond River. I decided to shelter behind the horseshoe-shaped Middleton Reef until the bad weather abated, and then try the deep-sea gear in nearby deep water beyond the continental shelf.

Looking for reefs in bad weather is always a stressful job as one has to remain alert, but I found it on this windy, rainy, miserable afternoon. When we had anchored safely, I went to my bunk for a sleep, only to be woken by Mano Totau, who said there was a mirror flashing from a wreck some three miles along the horseshoe reef. We suspected some wreck survivors were trying to signal us. Was it a coincidence that Mano, whom I had rescued from the island of 'Ata in 1966, should spot other survivors to be rescued from a reef in 1974?

Mano was anxious to launch the workboat immediately and investigate the mirror flashes. However, I told him to leave it until the next day because of the rain and wind and late afternoon conditions. "After all," I said, "whoever they are, they have drinking water for the night because it's raining heavily."

Next morning at dawn, Mano was ready to go with two helpers. They saw the remains of a wooden Japanese or Korean long liner in the distance but had to wade towards it across the top of a large expanse of coral reef at half-tide, towing the floating workboat behind them. They stopped here and there to stuff their tummies with some delicious clams and sea urchins, which abounded on top of the reef.

Eventually they arrived at the wreck to meet four starving New Zealanders who were on their last can of baked beans and too afraid to venture out on the reef for fear of sharks. Their fanciful story can best be gleaned from the press releases reproduced on the following pages.

The very hungry Welsh/New Zealand skipper told me he had built the Ferro cement boat, *Sospan Fach*, with a flush deck upon which he bolted a couple of park benches with steel frames. On one of these benches, he had mounted a gimballed magnetic compass.

Their voyage started in Auckland sailing north to North Cape, whereupon they turned left and headed west according their magnetic compass towards Australia. However, they must have sailed northwest to wreck the yacht on Middleton Reef.

The owner/skipper assured me he was sailing west because he claimed he had checked their compass course as they headed into the winter sunset. He did not realise that the sun does not set in the west in midwinter, but northwest; nor did he take into account how the iron in the park bench to which his magnetic compass was fastened would have affected the compass needle.

By actually sailing northwest from New Zealand, he had hit Middleton Reef. The helmsman said he did not see the breakers in the moon's path. By the time we arrived, the remains of the Ferro cement yacht had broken up and looked like a sunken cement footpath in the shallow, clear waters of the reef. The survivors had taken shelter on a nearby wreck, the Japanese tuna fishing boat *Fuku Maru*,[1] on which they had lived as castaways for six weeks.

The wrecked *Fuku Maru*

On board the MV *Ata*, the four survivors quickly regained their strength with good food and rest. However, the deeply distressed owner/skipper remained permanently at the mess table as if fearful of missing any morsel of food.

Christine Braham, an attractive girl from Adelaide, kept a diary and said, "We hardly talked for the whole six weeks on the wreck," as morale degenerated.

It seemed that no effort had been made to keep a permanent fire alight even though the wreck was a wooden ship. There was plenty of copper piping in the hulk's refrigeration system but no one had attempted to build a still to make fresh water.

---

[1] Wrecked in November 1963, all 26 crew were rescued by a sister ship, the *Dai Maru*, and taken to Brisbane.

Captain Irfon Nicholas of the ill-fated *Sospan Fach*

It is possible that as their hunger increased, the castaways may have become more innovative in their desperation; but I was surprised that they had not ventured onto the reef at low water to enjoy the abundant delicacies growing there.

The two young girls seemed to be coping with their situation, but I could see no evidence of leadership qualities in the owner or any idea amongst the men of even the most elementary survival skills. From my personal observations, I estimated they would have been dead within another month as food, fresh water and matches were exhausted.

After boarding the survivors, and whilst still at anchor in the horseshoe anchorage of Middleton Reef, we radioed ahead with the news of the rescue. By the time we arrived back to the port at Ballina, a huge contingent of reporters had gathered, to each create the most sensational report for their media bosses. The press even interviewed my wife in Sydney before I arrived back in Ballina. One newspaper described me as "The quiet hero of the reef". Many of my close friends teased me about this for years.

Skipper of the MV *Ata*, Peter Warner, & his wife Justine
(*The Sun* 13 June 1974)

The following is the text of the article reporting the rescue of the *Sospan Fach* skipper and crew as it appeared in *The Sun* 13 June 1974.

THE QUIET HERO OF THE REEF

This is how Mrs Justine Warner, mother of three, spoke today of her husband, Peter, who found the castaways on Middleton reef. Mrs Warner spoke at her Cammeray home while preparing her family—two girls and a boy, aged 13, 12 and 7—for school.

Mrs Warner said she saw her husband last Friday before he flew from Sydney to Ballina. His fishing trawler Ata had been refitted at Swan Bay, Richmond River, and had been sailed to Ballina before setting sail on its present cruise.

"It was supposed to be just another fishing trip," said Mrs Warner. She had not received any message since the rescue. "But I expect he'll ring me as soon as he gets into Ballina," she added.

The Ata with the two girls and two men saved from the wrecked yacht *Sospan Fach* is due in Ballina on Sunday. The survivors are Irfon Nicholas, 35, Christine Braham, 23, of Adelaide, Peter Lindemeyer, 18, of Melbourne, and Geraldine York, 19, of Auckland.

SECRET FOOD ON 'GHOST SHIP'

A survivor of a previous wreck said today there was a secret cache of food and water on Middleton Reef. But the shipwrecked crew of the *Sospan Fach* could not reach it. They did not know it was there—and probably would have drowned trying to reach it.

The emergency stores were placed in the wrecked freighter *Runic* three years ago by Sydney Mr Peter Dabbs. He was skipper of the ketch *One And All*, which foundered off the reef several days later.

Mr Dabbs—one of the few men in Sydney ever to visit the remote reef—said today he put 10 gallons of fresh water in a sealed drum and a quantity of tinned food in the wheelhouse of the *Runic* for just such an emergency as the *Sospan Fach*.

"But they wouldn't have been able to reach it," he said. "They took refuge on the other wreck, a Japanese fishing trawler. "To get to the *Runic* they would have had to walk 12 miles around the reef—and you can only do that at low tide. "It's a slow walk and the tide would probably get anyone trying to make it."

Mr Dabbs said only the two wrecked ships are above water at high tide. A big surf constantly pounds the reef. The waters are alive with sharks, sea snakes and deadly stonefish.

Mr Dabbs described the reef as desolate, but also as one of the most beautiful places he has seen.

REEF-WRECK FOUR LIFTED OFF

Sydney. The four survivors of the wrecked yacht *Sospan Fach* are expected to reach the NSW coast on Sunday. They are aboard a Tongan trawler, the *Ata*, which rescued them from Middleton Reef, 170 miles north of Lord Howe Island, yesterday.

The *Ata*'s owner, Mr Peter Warner, plans to put the four ashore at Ballina on the NSW coast, 500 miles north of Sydney.

The survivors are Peter Lindenmayer, 18, of Balwyn: Christine Braham, 25, of Adelaide, the yacht's skipper, Welshman Irfon Nicholas, 35, and Geraldine York, 19, of NZ.

They were found on the reef, where they had lived since 28 April, by the *Ata* which reported they were safe and well on Monday night.

Peter Lindenmayer's mother, Mrs Graeme Lindenmayer, in Melbourne last night said she would fly to Ballina on Sunday to meet her son.

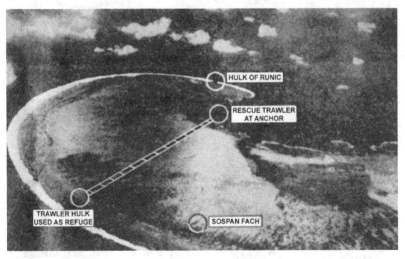

Middleton Reef, 170 miles north of Lord Howe Island, taken from a plane, which flew over the area yesterday (*The Sun*, Thursday, 13 June 1974)

The Australian Women's Weekly devoted their front page and five more pages to the story, some of which are reproduced in part or in full on the following pages.

THE AUSTRALIAN
Women's Weekly

June 26, 1974 / July 10, 1974

25c◆
New Zealand 30c
New Guinea 50c
Malaysia $1.50

REEF RESCUE
Stories and
color pictures
Pages 2, 3, 7, 8, 9

Booklet of Family Knits ● Gift wrappings
to make ● Serial: "An Accident of Love"
● Joan Sutherland — exclusive interview

Scene on deck in the Japanese fishing boat. Supplies left by the fishermen, and by a later salvage party, had been ruined by fire

Tongan crewmen bring Irfon Nicholas (wading, left) and Peter Lindenmayer to the MV *Ata*; Mano Totau pulling dinghy.

MOST OF THE PICTURES on these pages were taken by one of the men on the trawler *Ata*—an Australian shipwright and engineer, Bill York, who works at Swan Bay, near Ballina. He is a friend of the *Ata*'s owner, and he sailed with him from Ballina a few days previously, to test some new fishing gear. It was during this trip that the trawler ran into a storm and took shelter in the lee of Middleton Reef ... and made the rescue of *Sospan Fach*'s skipper and crew

Rescued group in the MV *Ata*, about to be landed at last at Ballina, NSW

7. Middleton Reef

THE DROPOUT WHO WENT TO SEA

PETER WARNER, owner of the Tongan trawler which made the Middleton Reef rescue, ran away from his wealthy home at 17 . . . and later learned Swedish to sit for his master's certificate. KAY KEAVNEY interviewed him at Ballina.

"I'D PREFER to fight nature rather than human beings," said Peter Warner.

He said it quietly, even with a hint of self-mockery, summing up both himself and his life.

Peter Warner is the now legendary skipper-owner of the Ata, part of his fleet of five fishing boats and two freighters, Tonga-based.

Ata, the Polynesian name of a certain island, means "the twilight before the dawn."

Earlier that morning, in the milky half light before dawn, Captain Warner had been preparing to bring Ata over the storm-tossed bar into Ballina with the four people from the wrecked yacht Sospan Fach.

That bar is dangerous, especially in such weather. First light is one of the few favorable times to cross it.

Peter Warner had radioed from Middleton Reef, 320 miles away, on the preceding Friday that he would cross it precisely then; at first light on this Monday morning.

He had made so many rescues that when he saw the Sospan Fach survivors, he said to himself, laughing, ''Oh no! Not again!''

"And he'll do it," said the old salts in the waiting crowd. "Bang on schedule."

"He's a marvellous sailor," said one.

He did it, bang on schedule, just as the last stars paled. He hadn't even been about outside, but had timed it exactly, along with doing a little fishing on the long voyage.

In all the madness of the welcome, he'd stayed on his little bridge, unruffled, unfailingly courteous, thick-sweatered, bareheaded, with laughter lines deep-etched round very blue seaman's eyes.

Now, that night, he was dining by candlelight with photographer Keith Barlow and me in a Ballina restaurant.

He looked urbane in jacket and tie, expertly choosing the wine. This was the other aspect of Peter Warner, privileged son of Sir Arthur Warner, electronics tycoon, former Victorian cabinet minister and Leader of the Upper House on the conservative side.

"I didn't have a tie," he told us, the laughter lines etched deeper. "I tried to borrow one from the (mostly Tongan) crew. The cabin boy was the only one on board who owned one, so I purloined it."

He touched the neat knot. What drove Peter Warner? What made him tick?

Here was a man who'd tossed it all in to go adventuring, to go to sea, to take off his lot and get away from "getting and spending."

Somewhere, willy-nilly, adventure had kept tapping him on the shoulder.

He had saved so many lives that when, through binoculars, he had spied the Sospan Fach survivors on the wrecked Japanese trawler on the reef, he had said to himself, laughing, "Oh no! Not again!"

He poured the wine, and splendid seafood appeared on the candle-lit table, but he chose a thick steak. He'd been living off seafood ever since his three-day voyage to test new fishing equipment changed to a protracted rescue operation.

He was the younger of two brothers, he said, and pretty much the family odd-man-out.

"My brother," he said with affection, "is a scientist, the studious type, the original absent-minded professor."

Their father, the late Sir Arthur, had many business interests.

Their big home was at Brighton, Victoria, and Peter sailed from as far back as he can remember.

(Later, he had a distinguished career in races like the Hobart Yacht Race, taking fine honors in his vessel, Astor, in which he also sailed many thousands of Pacific miles.)

"I was always interested in a physical challenge," he said. "If you like, I was always interested in cowboys and Indians. As a child, I loved the old Viking stories.

"I loved things like boxing and swimming. But I remember giving up boxing, giving it up completely, because I knocked somebody's teeth out."

He paused a while.

"I became fascinated," he went on, "with the study of survival as a youngster, when I tipped over a small sailing boat and stupidly tried to swim ashore. Fortunately, someone had spotted me from the shore, and I was rescued.

"From then on, I studied human survival, both in a practical way and academically. My hobby is still navigating without instruments, using the old ways common in the islands. I love studying the old ships . . . and astronomy . . .

"When I was 17, I ran away to sea.

"My father caught me when I sailed home a year later, and made me matriculate, then enrol in Law at the University of Melbourne.

"After six weeks of Law I ran away to sea again.

"This time I made it for three whole years. I served in the Swedish and Norwegian navies and fishing fleets. I learnt to speak Swedish . . . in fact, I did all my exams for my papers in Swedish.

"After three years I came home sporting my Swedish master's ticket. But my father wanted for me — well, something other than the sea.

"So I asked him, 'What's easiest?'

"'My father,' said. 'Accountancy.' You know, that wasn't true!

"Anyway, for the next five years I worked in his business by day and studied accountancy at night."

Peter eased his tie with a finger.

"Well, after five years of this I was a public accountant, working for my father.

"I had a very broad experience in business.

"But it lost its challenge by the time I was 35. Meanwhile, I'd got married.

"Her name's Justine. She's a beautiful Irish-looking brunette with blue eyes, of Scottish extraction. She's a very good artist.

"I loved the old Viking stories"

"In fact, she's a good all-rounder.

"She lived just a few blocks away.

"I explained to Justine that this was my last fling.

"I was away five months and got back two days before the wedding. In my youth I'd worked on Swedish ships doing the Australia-Japan run. And I talked us into a berth on one of these ships — the 'hospital' berth — for a honeymoon. It was marvellous. It lasted five months."

Both badly wanted a family, but they were childless for six years.

"Six miscarriages, one after the other," he said very soberly. "Then a premature baby who lived a few days. I couldn't put her through it again. We adopted our much-loved Carolyn, now 13. We owe Carolyn everything. Three months later, Justine was pregnant with Janet (now 11). Peter (now seven) was born in Tonga."

Round about 1960, the family had moved from Melbourne to Sydney, with Peter still yoked to business.

"I opened a small fleet of crayfishing boats, based in Tasmania. When I got really fed up with business, I went fishing to regain my sanity.

"I don't mind," he exploded, "fighting villains

Tongans gave fishing secrets

and thieves and rogues, but not bureaucrats!"

He tugged at the tie.

Year by year, he reached as fields were fished out. Constantly, he searched for new fishing grounds. In this search, in 1966, he sailed one of his fleet to Tongan waters.

"I was carrying all the latest, most sophisticated European fishing equipment," he said, "but we just couldn't catch those crayfish!

"One day, we had our traps set on a reef about four miles from an uninhabited island called Ata.

"Idly, I turned my binoculars on its rugged, volcanic island, and saw a burnt-out patch on a cliff. So we went to investigate.

"Down the cliff ran a naked youth. Others followed, yelling. They were so wild that the crew started looking at our guns."

In this first famous rescue, he restored to their parents six schoolboys (still ranging only from 14 years to 18) from Tonga, who had marooned on a boat 15 months before for a night's illicit fishing and been carried away by storms.

They fascinated the student of survival.

"Two of the elder youths emerged as natural leaders, holding absolute sway over the others. All societies seem to begin like that, with the emergence of born aristocrats."

Later, some of the boys joined his crew. One, Mano Totau (of whom young Peter Lindenmayer was to say, "Mano's the hero. He saved us"), was part of the Sospan Fach's rescue party.

In Tonga, Peter Warner was feasted and feted. And every feast happened to sport lavish helpings of crayfish. The islanders had succeeded where others with all their fishing equipment had failed!

In gratitude to the saviour of their sons and heirs, the Tongans promised to share the secrets of their fishing grounds and methods.

Then Peter approached his wife about moving to Tonga.

So the Warners moved to Tonga (though keeping their Cammeray, Sydney, house). They live near the royal palace.

Justine started to love the life.

"Pretty soon," Peter said, "she was running the local art society, and the Red Cross, and the bridge clubs, and setting up the first bookshop in Tonga."

Peter junior was born. He could swim like a fish almost before he could walk.

"For years," said his father, "his was the only white bottom among the brown ones."

Adventure, for little Peter, first meant sneaking into the royal palace nearby.

By then, Queen Salote was dead, and her successor was the Queen Consort Maataho, very stately and well over 6ft. tall.

"Around then, I'd been trying to teach Peter the difference between truth and a lie.

"This morning, when he was all of three, he got away from his Tongan nanny, sneaked past the guards, and got into the palace, and ran right into the stately queen.

"She said, 'Who are you?'

"He said, 'I'm Peter Warner. Who are you?'

"Her Majesty said, 'I am Queen Maataho.'

"And Peter looked up at her and barked, 'Truth or a lie?'"

This year, young Peter and his sunbrowned sisters — with their mother — have gone back to the Cammeray house to be educated in Australian schools.

As often as he can, Peter Warner flies home to Sydney, as he did this month. Then, on to Ballina and the Richmond River, where Ata (named after the island of that first rescue operation) was being reconverted as a fishing vessel.

What now for Peter Warner?

In answer, Peter talked of his beloved Polynesians.

"They love and know the sea as few Europeans do. Theirs are undeveloped countries. My present dream is to develop the Polynesian sea-farming capabilities into a Norway of the Pacific," he said.

"I think the Polynesians can become the seafarers and harvesters of the Pacific."

PETER WARNER

The Australian Women's Weekly — June 26, 1974/July 10, 1974

Page 7

The Australian Women's Weekly, 26 June–10 July 1974, page 7
(see text in Appendix 1)

The sea trial voyage had been successful. To escape further publicity, we quickly refuelled and victualed the ship, and departed hastily from Ballina to Tonga.

8
Ma'afu Enterprises
and loss of the *Just David*

8
Ma'afu Enterprises
and loss of the *Just David*

The US Peace Corp was established by President Kennedy in the 1960s as an attempt to offer and teach the so-called benefits of US ideals to third world countries via young US volunteers. In Tonga, the starry-eyed team of young volunteers was directed by Layton Zimmer, whose family became close friends of mine. Young teachers, carpenters, farmers and other skilled young US volunteers were paid $US32 per month to live in a remote village and assist the locals.

Our fishing boat, FV *Just David*, was chartered by the Director to drop the volunteers onto outer islands where the locals provided grass hut accommodation and local food. Many of these young people succumbed to dysentery and diarrhoea for the first few months whilst the locals cared for them. The volunteers learned a lot but I am not sure the Tongans got much out of it. When I asked the locals, why the volunteers came to live and work with them, most thought it was for the money.

$US32 was a lot of money in the eyes of the Tongans at that time! Others thought the youngsters came to avoid compulsory military conscription in the US. I had an agronomist volunteer helping me with a taro planting exercise, but later he was arrested for growing marijuana somewhere. My daughters and I used to deliver some good food to him on Sundays whilst he was in Toli Toli prison. The girls were shocked at the poor conditions in this lockup.

Layton Zimmer retired after his tour of duty and stayed in Tonga to set up a partnership with me known as Ma'afu Enterprises which provided tours for foreign tourists and transport for all-comers. Tourists, missionaries, bureaucrats and others wanting to visit some of the 177 islands in Tonga needed transport. To be in Tonga without a boat was like being in outback Australia without a vehicle or camel or horse.

Brochure front page

CAPTAIN COOK'S DISCOVERY TOURS: Board a large, modern, GLASS-BOTTOM BOAT for an off-shore tour of historic Nuku'alofa and a close viewing of the lovely harbour reefs and the sea life at home there. Then explore Mu'a passage, tracing the route taken by Captain Cook in 1773 when he first landed on Tongan soil. The tour route includes the present King's summer residence and many landmarks of ancient Tonga. Lunch and/or refreshments will be served on board, depending on the length of the tour and the time of day. If visitors wish, the limousines of TETA Tours will be available to continue the tour on land around the most historic villages and monuments on the eastern end of Tongatapu Island. All tours (half day or whole day, by sea or by land and sea) return to Nuku'alofa with plenty of time to explore Tonga's capital city and to consider the handicrafts and duty-free goods available there. Local bookings for harbour tours and for Sundowner and Moonlight party cruises and for special picnic or fishing trips are accepted through TETA Tours at the International Dateline Hotel (P. O. Box 215, Nuku'alofa, Tonga, South Pacific.)

MA'AFU ENTEPRISES

P. O. BOX 132, NUKU'ALOFA.
KINGDOM OF TONGA, SOUTH PACIFIC
CABLE "MA'AF TOURS" TONGA.

Tonga was named THE FRIENDLY ISLANDS by Captain Cook almost 200 years ago. Well named!—and it still applies today. The kindness, good humour and hospitality of a Tongan welcome continues to amaze and please guests from all over the world. The spirit of Tonga is beyond price, for instance, tipping is quite unnecessary—but we do hope for the visitor's understanding and concern for the way of life here. Modesty of dress is greatly appreciated in Tonga. Bikinis are fine for beaches and boat decks; muumuus, shifts or pants suits for women and sports shirts and walking shorts for men are suitable in towns or island villages. For most of the year, the weather is as warm as the welcome in the Friendly Islands of Tonga, informality and a smile are the keys to enjoyment Visit us, relax and see.

Brochure back page

My contribution to the partnership Ma'afu Enterprises was the use of FV *Just David*. Layton provided his time to operate the business. I was otherwise occupied with fishing and freighting and did not wish to be catering to the many whims of travellers. My tolerance was limited. It was better to keep me away from pedantic pale-faced passengers who asked stupid questions. Layton was far more patient!

FV *Just David*

With time to spare in between charters to foreign visitors, Layton ran a local passenger service between Nuku'alofa and Eua, a big high island to the East of Tongatapu. By 1973, Mano Totau had progressed from schoolboy runaway to holding a Captain's certificate for small coastal vessels. He was in charge of FV *Just David* in June 1973 on a 20-mile voyage to Eua. An artificial harbour had been built on the western side of this steep-to island of limestone cliffs.

On this fateful voyage, the regular easterly trade wind had been replaced by a westerly fresh breeze creating large waves, which were breaking into and across the small entrance of the artificial harbour. Mano stopped the boat and waited outside the entrance for a break between the waves. He knew that often after three big waves there was a lull.

Many of the deck passengers were ladies with babies and children in their arms. Most were sea sick and crying to Mano to get them into the harbour quickly. Nervously he waited and, after one series of three waves, he surfed ahead to the entrance with the fresh wind behind him. Unfortunately, a fluke wave lifted the stern of *Just David* and crashed it onto the rocks on one side of the harbour entrance where it quickly pounded to pieces. Deck passengers and their children were thrown into the boiling sea by the impact. A brave young policeman from onshore jumped into the boiling sea to affect some rescues but was himself drowned in the attempt. Altogether six lives were lost. Most of them were young children and babies plus the policeman.

Mano and the remainder of the passengers finally made it ashore. It is strange that I had rescued Mano with his five companions five years earlier and was now involved with the loss of an equal number of Tongans at Eua. God works in strange ways. We all grieved for this sad loss of young people.

Some local would-be lawyers told the families to sue me for the loss of life, as I was the owner of the boat. Fortunately, I was protected with limited liability provided by the Tongan Shipping Act of the day. However, at a preliminary trial by one of the claimants, a local judge offered a wise remark to everybody, by asking how one can measure grief with money. After that the claims were dropped.

FV *Just David* was not insured and there was no replacement handy, so Ma'afu Enterprises closed its doors and the Zimmer family returned to the US where Layton renewed his work as an Episcopalian minister. Mano lost his Captain's certificate and went on to other adventures, utilizing his cooking skills, to become a well-known chef in Tonga.

I had lost my beloved *Just David*, built in 1956 and named after my wife and the son of a partner in a crayfishing venture in Apollo Bay, Victoria. After winding up that partnership, I had taken *Just David* for a refit for new work in Tasmania with cabins installed for six passengers. Amongst other ventures, she serviced the lighthouses at Maatsuyker and Tasman Islands. Thus, with her reliable Gardner engine, *Just David* was a well-travelled, trustworthy boat, and had become renowned all the way from stormy Tasmania to Tonga.

Sometimes my family with friends had used her for little voyages of pleasure. Our very good friends, Inoke (later 'Akau'ola) and 'Evelini Faletau, with their six kids would join Justine and me and our three kids on short weekend voyages to nearby uninhabited islands. The crew would land a barrel of water, rig up a temporary hut and start a fire. The kids frolicked on the shore and in the shallows. Inoke and I would venture out onto the reef and sit in the shallows to devour *tuku misi*, a type of sea egg with brown spikes. It contains a yellow caviar-type roe, which is claimed to be an aphrodisiac and is also deliciously tasty.

Come the evening the pressure lantern would be lit and the cards brought out to enjoy many hours of contract bridge on a rug whilst the children slept all around us.

'Evelini and Inoke Faletau (later Honourable 'Akau'ola)

There are no snakes in Tonga, except banded sea snakes, which have a habit of coming out of the sea and are attracted to the warmth of a fire. They cannot do much harm because their mouth is too small to bite an adult; but all snakes are scary to Tongans and also to my wife.

In the midst of a hand of bridge, 'Evelini glanced at our fire outside the hut and let out a loud scream as she saw snakes gathered close by. That was the end of the bridge game. The ladies commanded us back on board immediately to escape the snakes. The camp had to be abandoned until morning and we all paddled out to the *Just David* to sleep in bunks. I have many fond memories of this little wooden ship.

9
The Tongan Royal family

9
The Tongan Royal family

To understand a little about how the pecking order functions in Tongan society and some of the unusual customs of Tongans and the land laws, one first has to appreciate the power of the present line of rulers.

When I first arrived in 1966, Tonga operated as a feudal state, but was also toying around with the edges of democracy. Democracy may or may not be the solution for this, and other very tribal societies. Like most of us, the Tongans crave for a strong firm leader. They have little respect for weak leaders, whether a king or a noble or town officer. History shows us that civilization develops from family unity to tribal unity to state unity, thence to commonwealth or federations and finally to world unity. Some advanced societies are attempting to achieve the latter in the form of the United Nations.

Many describe the Kingdom of Tonga as a benevolent dictatorship living in a well-fed poverty. Although well intentioned, sometimes the king's wish overrode published statutes of parliament. When His Majesty said jump, the only question allowed was how high. This was confusing for me because I had always been taught to obey the law of the land in which one resided, even before I became a Bahá'í.

I remember my first practical experience of this phenomenon in the early 1970s when I was operating some fishing-cum-passenger boats registered under the Tongan Shipping Act (which was a copy of a very early British Act). One day, the King issued a directive in Council, which was in contradiction to a section in the Shipping Act.

His Majesty's command adversely affected my passenger business. I went to the then Chief Justice, Harry Roberts, and asked him what was more important, the clause in the written statute or the King's decree. Judge Roberts said the statute law overrode the King's wish and recommended I follow the written law.

I went then to my Tongan advisors and asked them the same question. They asked, "Peter do you like living in Tonga?" to which I answered, "Yes of course."

"OK," they said, "in that case, just do what the King says,"—so I did.

Of course the royal family were, and are, top of the pecking order, followed by 32 nobles of the realm who control 32 estates. Some members of the royal family have additional estates and the government holds the remaining land—which is not much—as crown land.

No one can buy freehold land. The nobles can lease part of their estates to foreigners but are obliged to allocate and register allotments in their estates to all their commoners.

King Tupou I

Before the present line of royalty took control of Tonga in the early 19th century, the rulers of Tonga were divided into warrior kings and spiritual kings. Coinciding with the arrival of Christian missionaries, the warrior leaders disposed of the spiritual leaders (Tui Tonga line).

9. The Tongan Royal family

Tupou I (the First) and his father finally annihilated the Tui Tonga line in a battle at Pea in 1817. He was baptized as George in 1831 and was the first in the line to be crowned, as represented in the following order:

	Born	Crowned	Died	Age
Tupou I	1798	1845	1893	95
Tupou II	1874	1893	1918	43
Queen Sālote	1900	1918	1966	66
Tupou IV	1918	1967	2006	88
Tupou V	1948	2008	2012	64
Tupou VI	1959	2015		

Tupou I and his father were ruthless warrior leaders from the Ha'apai group of islands in the middle of Tonga. Tupou I unified his 177 island kingdom by conquest in the same way that Genghis Khan unified tribal Mongolia. He was a thin tall active man, ate plenty of fish, and lived until he was at least 90 years old when his death was allegedly caused by eating a poisonous fish. It is said that he witnessed the sacking of the British Privateer Port au Prince as a young man in 1806 on the island of Lifuka in Ha'apai. The Tongans burned the ship, leaving only a few survivors including William Mariner who later published his story in London in 1817. Mariner lived with the family of Tupou I for about four years until a passing whaler rescued him and returned him to Britain. Mariner said Tupou I and his family were determined rulers.

His Royal Highness (HRH) Crown Prince Tupouto'a (later Tupou V) told me that Tupou I witnessed how much better the Christian foreigners were at killing their enemies; more deadly than the Tongans who had only their stone-headed clubs and arrows. According to HRH, who often related very colourful stories, Tupou I had the notion that he and his people would become better at killing if they all became Christians. He also figured that since he and his Dad had annihilated the opposition spiritual leaders in battle, wholesale Christian conversion of his people would help to silence any remnants of the old religion.

So he ordered the whole population to become Christian or be clubbed to death; and he had himself baptized George in 1831. I hasten to add that HRH the Crown Prince Tupouto'a, who told me this story, had a unusual sense of humour and openly questioned many aspects of the Wesleyan Church, which is one of the leading Christian churches in Tonga. (More about this in the chapter devoted to HRH.)

During his long reign, Tupou I managed to maintain Tonga's independence from European colonization. Tonga and Brunei are the only two Asia-Pacific countries that remained independent of foreign powers, albeit later becoming British Protectorates until after World War II when full nationhood status was granted by Britain.

A Protectorate can best be described where locals administer all internal matters and the Protector attends to all foreign affairs. The wily Tupou I was able to achieve independence for Tonga by playing one foreign power off against the other. He was always keen to enter into treaties of friendship with whichever power had the biggest navy in the area at the time. Although not educated in the European sense, he was a born diplomat. The following story demonstrates this.

Tupou II

As mentioned in Chapter 2, the Christian missionaries who were infiltrating Tonga at the time insisted that the local nobles and their warrior sons and nephews stop fighting one another and try living in peace.

Deprived of a good fight at home the hyperactive youths took to sailing down to the eastern islands of Fiji known as the Lau group to burn, rape and pillage a few villages. In their very fast and large catamaran-style canoes known as *kalia*, they could run with the wind behind them 200 miles from the south of Tonga to the Lau group within

24 hours, cause havoc and then tight reach back to the northern islands of Vavau Tonga all within 72 hours.

Tiring of this sport the Tongans then started to settle a number of the Lau group islands, which were given Tongan names. A half-brother of Tupou I, Maʻafu, had taken up residence on the island of Lakemba in the Lau group.

The Fijian chiefs wanted Her Britannic Majesty Queen Victoria to colonize Fiji for fear that Tongans may invade the whole Fiji group and take over. The Melanesian Fijians perceived the Polynesian Tongans as thieving, untrustworthy villains and some still do.

Sometime after the Fijian chiefs petitioned Queen Victoria, the British Government finally sent a gunboat around the Fijian islands to obtain the signatures or marks of all the Fijian chiefs onto the ceding document. However, upon arriving at Lakemba, Maʻafu refused to sign, claiming that the Lau group was occupied and part of Tonga. Undaunted, the British took Maʻafu in the gunboat back to his half-brother in Tonga. The chief British negotiator is alleged to have said to Tupou I, "If you don't persuade your brother Maʻafu to sign this ceding document, we will withdraw our protection of Tonga and let other European powers interfere and colonise Tonga."

Tupou I had a quiet word with his brother and explained that it would be smarter for Tonga to give up its claim to the Lau group rather than lose control of all 177 home islands of Tonga. Of course Maʻafu had to agree to this sacrifice and it is reported he died broken hearted three months later.

On a visit to Sydney, Tupou I observed the destitute conditions of the aborigines who had been chased off their lands and reduced to a state of degradation. Determined that this would never happen in Tonga, he made sure, when granting his constitution in 1875, that no foreigners would ever own land in Tonga.

Today all the land is still owned by the King, but divided into 32 estates, each administered by a noble. Nobles may only lease up to 5% off their estates to foreigners. In my time in Tonga, every elder son had both a town allotment for a house and a bush allotment sufficient for rotational organic cropping.

In my opinion, the work and foresight of Tupou I launched Tonga into the most secure position in order to retain its dignity, independence and wellbeing as it moved forward into a tumultuous period of Pacific history. Without him, Tonga would have become just another European colony later granted independence without a firm leader. Witness the mess of governments throughout the remainder of Pacific island nations.

So Tonga was blessed by the unity established over 177 islands, a constitution protecting its land, and the benefits of Christianity, which taught that there was only one God for everybody thus introducing the concept of love into a previously pagan religion.

In my view, his only fault was allowing the Methodist (Wesleyan) missionaries to draft his constitution. Amongst other matters, it states that the Sabbath shall be holy and no entertainment, games, work or sport are to be allowed on Sundays. The only thing allowed on Sundays is attending Church, feasting and making babies.

This restricted the activities of us foreigners who wanted to play on Sundays. Sometimes, when my wife occasionally became fed up with Tonga, she would bundle the kids into the mini moke and head for the beach on a Sunday afternoon. On one occasion she announced, "I don't care if the police catch me and deport me." Fortunately, this never happened.

Tupou I left the throne to one of his grandchildren, Tupou II, who liked European alcohol. He had a benign reign of 25 years and died at the early age of 43. He was an accomplished musician as were all future royals. He may have fared better if he had stuck to the national drink of kava. Whilst the kava root contains a strong narcotic, the drink that is made from the plant is a hypnotic. Kava is an acquired taste, and brings to mind the muddy colour of a flooded river. It slowly induces a feeling of wellbeing and makes one loquacious and amorous—not like alcohol, which makes many violent.

Queen Sālote (Charlotte) was the third sovereign of the line. Crowned at the age of 18, she was the daughter of Tupou II by his first wife, Queen Lavinia, who had died of tuberculosis. With no male heir resulting from the king's second marriage, Sālote was the best choice in most people's opinion. The excellent book written by Elizabeth Wood Ellem published in 1981, titled *"Queen Sālote of Tonga"*, gives a detailed account of her appointment and life.

One of her claims to fame was her insistence on riding in the rain in an open carriage at the coronation of Her Britannic Majesty Queen Elizabeth II in London. Queen Sālote was a grand and large lady over six foot tall. Her open carriage was shared with the small Monarch of Ethiopia, Haile Selassie, who later developed the flu from this experience.

Sir Laurence Olivier, the famous English actor, had rented a balcony with a good view along the procession route. He invited Noel Coward and other well-known actors to share the balcony view with him. As Queen Sālote's carriage passed in the rain, Laurence Olivier asked, "Who is that riding with the Queen of Tonga?"

Noel Coward replied, "That is her lunch!" to the merriment of those present and retold on many later occasions. The son of Laurence Olivier, Tarquin Olivier, who was there as a small boy and witnessed it all, confirmed the details of this story when I met him later.

Tarquin visited Tonga several times as a representative of Delarue, security printers who supplied Tonga's bank notes for many years. I got to know him quite well.

Queen Sālote Tupou III

I first arrived in Tonga not long after Her Majesty's death. The country was still in mourning. Everyone wore black from head to toe for 12 months. I believe she became more popular and loved as she grew older, but cancer got the better of her at 65.

Then came Tupou IV (HM) who ruled whilst I was in Tonga. His coronation was in 1967 and he ruled until his death in 2006. He lived longer than we all expected because he was so heavy and appeared to have trouble breathing.

When I first met Tupou IV, he weighed 28 stone, but later reduced himself to 26 stone. He was tall and must have been a challenging rugby opponent when he attended boarding school in Sydney and, later, when he attended Sydney University to obtain a law degree.

King Tupou IV 2004

As Crown Prince, he was given the title of Tungi. For many years, he oversaw government and royal enterprises including the Copra Board and Tonga Navigation, which operated a few government vessels. His brother, Tu'ipelahake, was the Prime Minister, so most of government was in royal hands.

After his Coronation, Tupou IV maintained a keen interest in trying to improve Tongan life for all. Education was a pet subject and teaching of mathematics was his particular hobby. All kids in government schools were instructed in the use of the abacus, which he described as an early form of computer used by the Chinese for centuries. One of my hobbies was also education and, in the 1970s, I thought the Cuisenaire rods were a better tool to teach mathematics rather than the abacus. At one of my audiences, I gave HM a set of Cuisenaire cubes and rods and demonstrated their use. A few days later, a Palace Office message summonsed me to an audience where HM declared the Cuisenaire rods as deficient because there was no cube or rod representing zero.

Amongst many ideas, the ever-active brain of His Majesty entertained a plan to use zeppelin-type airships to carry Tongan bananas from the growing islands direct to the produce market in Auckland thereby saving time and handling. At the time, two of my vessels were engaged in carrying Tongan bananas to the South Island of New Zealand, so HM gave me the task of undertaking a feasibility study of the airship plan. It did not take long to calculate that the project was not financially viable.

During an audience with HM in early 1970, I asked if I could register and fly the Tongan flag on the two Australian fishing boats that I had brought with me. I had previously acquired his permission to operate in Tongan waters.

"Yes," HM said. "Go and register them with the Registrar of Ships."

A New Zealander, Selwyn Jones, held this post as well as Collector of Customs. He also said "yes" but asked for 25% duty to import each vessel before registration, so I declined the offer.

Next time I had an audience with HM he asked if my boats were now flying the Tongan flag to which I replied to the affect that, "No Your Majesty, because the Collector of Customs wanted too much money." HM thought for a while and said that if I flew the Tongan flag, he could grant me a monopoly of the Tongan fishing grounds. I replied, "Thank you Your Majesty, I deeply appreciate your kind offer but Korean, Chinese, Japanese and Taiwanese vessels are already fishing in Tongan waters unmolested, so your kind offer was not an effective offer unless foreign poaching could be stopped or policed."

He sat very still on his large throne and after what seemed a long time said, "What if we made your boats the volunteer coast guard? You could mount guns on your boats and we could go 50/50 on the proceeds of any foreign vessels you confiscate. I could give you a Letter of Marque."

Whilst trying to comprehend this offer I asked what a Letter of Marque was. HM said, "It can best be described as similar to the letter given by Queen Elizabeth I to the famous privateer Drake and others, authorizing them to go and plunder and bring back the prizes to the Queen for a 50% reward."

The reader will appreciate that Tupou IV was very well read about many things, including history, and had a photographic memory. I went away to consider the offer and talk to my naval architect about the reinforcements needed to the forepeak of each vessel upon which to mount the guns.

Meanwhile Crown Prince Tupouto'a returned from a course in diplomacy at Oxford University to tell his father that Tonga should have its own navy, which would be more effective than a volunteer coastguard. He had persuaded the British Government to contribute two aluminum patrol boats, which were already on order for Tonga.

The Crown Prince explained all this to me and I was able to forget the idea of becoming a privateer. At the same time HM asked me to become an advisor to his new navy, which we will discuss in the chapter dedicated to this often misunderstood Royal who finally became King.

Meanwhile, back to Tupou IV—although regarded by some as the master of unrealistic and unattainable thought bubbles, not all his many schemes were unworkable. The plan to secure Minerva Reef as part of the Kingdom, albeit comical, was well thought out and executed, as narrated in the earlier chapter headed "Minerva Reefs".

Tupou IV set an example of regular exercise to encourage his overweight subjects to take up the practice. In his early life, he had been a surfer with a huge long surfboard acquired from Hawaii.

Later he took to climbing up and down the Palace stairs with lead weights in the pockets of a heavy waistcoat. We went snorkelling together at Hunga Tonga with a large entourage of minders and experienced divers to accompany him in the deep underwater world.

At that time, the overweight King, now in his thirties, needed two well-weighted diving belts to give him neutral buoyancy. With only one weighted belt, he still floated on the surface like a stranded whale—28 stone takes a lot of sinking.

In later years, he took to riding regularly on a solidly-constructed bicycle around the streets of Nuku'alofa followed by his army security team, running and sweating alongside their monarch. He was also very strong as foreigners found out when offered a flipper-sized handshake that nearly crushed any smaller hand.

A New Zealand doctor suggested a strict weight-reducing diet, which included only one potato per day. His Majesty explained to the doctor that potatoes were not grown in Tonga and the doctor asked what the equivalent to a potato was eaten there. HM said yams were consumed by the upper class instead of potatoes, whereupon the doctor struck one potato of the diet list and replaced it with one yam. HM went away happy because the smallest yam weighs over 2 kg.

All 400 lb of solid new King, Tupou IV in 1966

His Majesty's wife had only partial success in enforcing the king's diet, and he was often seen sneaking visits to the kitchen at dawn, even when he was residing at the Tongan High Commission in London.

'Evelini Faletau, the wife of the Tongan High Commissioner in London, recalls being sent secretly, without the knowledge of the Queen, to the corner shop to buy sweet oranges and lollies for HM.

He was supported by the very capable Queen Mata'aho who bore him four children, Tupouto'a (later Tupou V), Princess Pilolevu, Ma'atu who died as a young married man, and Aho'eitu, who is now Tupou VI. Both the King and the Queen were accomplished musicians, he on the six-string guitar and the zither, and she on the piano.

Behind his large commanding demeanour, he was a very well educated, impractical, and likeable king. The Palace gardens were maintained by machete-wielding prisoners from the jail, guarded by one warder armed with a baton. I shall always fondly remember HM walking through the Palace grounds chatting to the prisoners who included many serious criminals and even a murderer who had escaped the noose.

10
The eccentric Crown Prince

10
The eccentric Crown Prince

Since Europeans first arrived in the Pacific, many colourful characters, both local and foreign have been recorded from amongst the many islands. The most flamboyant and underestimated character that I have encountered in my many years of wandering was His Royal Highness, Crown Prince Tupouto'a, who later became His Majesty King George Tupou V.

In the early 1970s, the only commercial flights in and out of Tonga originated in Nadi or Suva in Fiji. One would be dumped by a major international carrier in the middle of the night into the so-called international waiting lounge at Nadi airport, which was really an open-sided windy terminal with hard wooden benches. There, one reclined until the flight to Tonga departed soon after dawn in a DC3 operated by Fiji Airways, sometimes referred to as "Fiji Scare ways". These old aircraft could land on the short grass runway at Fuamotu in Tonga with a small load of passengers and a big life raft secured in the middle of the passenger cabin.

On a return trip to Tonga sometime in the early 1970s, I was waiting patiently in the Nadi transit lounge when I spotted a lanky young Tongan man with extremely long hair taking up most of a long bench as he slept away.

I thought to myself, "That looks like Tupouto'a." But I was not sure until he roused himself and sat up. I had met His Royal Highness (HRH) and seen him before at the bar of the Nuku'alofa Club (strictly a male domain) and at official parties, but this was the first time that we had a lengthy chat in the depth of night, not surrounded by his many secretaries, flunkies, servants, or any of his fair-weather sycophantic friends.

I reintroduced myself and asked him where he had absented himself for such a long time away from Tonga. "Oxford," he replied in the most cultured upper crust English accent, "doing a course in diplomacy, but I failed one of the set exercises, Pita." He sometimes addressed me as

"Pita" with a long emphasis on the last syllable or alternatively by the Russian nickname he bestowed on me, "Trotsky". No doubt, his creative imagination conjured up plans of intrigue, where I plotted to overthrow the government of his father, His Majesty King Tupou IV.

At the time, HRH was in his early to mid-20s and enjoyed life internationally and within his idyllic enclave of Tonga. Beneath a seemingly laid-back attitude, a deep and insightful-minded Prince was developing. I asked him why he had failed the diplomacy test and he explained, "One of the students and I were set as rulers of two imaginary countries. The border between our two countries was traditionally a river. The river flooded and found a new course bulging into my opponent's territory. The question was how to resolve this issue. I grasped the opportunity and occupied the bulge with my imaginary troops and declared the new land as mine. However, this was not the right answer or solution. The right answer was to take my claim to the international court at The Hague, so I failed that one."

He sighed with glee. "Anyway," he continued, "my parents first sent me to Sandhurst Military College for a few years to learn how to fight wars and then to a diplomacy course at Oxford University to learn how to avoid wars, so I don't know really which course of action they wish me to follow."

No doubt, he had studied his father's annexation of Minerva Reef, mentioned earlier, and the many exploits of his ancestor's attempts at annexing island territories in Fiji (explained in the chapter on the Tongan royal family). This was all a very good grounding in the skills of diplomatic manoeuvring of which he became a master.

After a few hours of chatting, we boarded our dawn flight and HRH disappeared into first class whilst I took up my economy seat together with the large life raft as company. We arrived safely and, the next time I saw him, I noticed that the Queen had commanded her young though her eldest son to have a serious short back and side haircut.

The exploits of a daredevil young prince continued. After a few high-speed car escapades, Their Majesties commanded him not to take the wheel of any more cars; so he bought a very powerful motorbike, which he rode up and down Vuna Road along the waterfront at hair-raising speed.

At that time, I had a diminutive Scottish engineer on my payroll called Jock Maestri (Scottish mother and Italian father). Jock hailed from Glasgow and HRH called this little imp "the Poisoned Dwarf". I think the name referred to a Scottish regiment, members of which served with HRH whilst policing the border between West and East Germany during part of his Sandhurst training.

"I get seasick in my bathtub." Tupouto'a in his Admiral's uniform

Jock was very skilful at tuning motorbikes to release maximum power. HRH commandeered him from my services for a while and one could witness the high-speed charges down Vuna Road with the imposing figure of the Crown Prince in front of a clinging little Scotsman hugging the rear saddle.

Unfortunately, the episode ended when the future king and the wee Scot sped into the wet terrazzo foyer entrance of the New Date Line Hotel and skidded. The bike went in one direction and HRH and the Scot ended up in another direction, coming to a halt amongst the manicured greenery. A bleeding Crown Prince emerged from the shrubbery and looked at the red blood oozing from his scratches. He was heard to remark ruefully in his refined English accent, "I'm afraid Royal blood is not blue."

That was the end of the major motorbike adventures although the machine was sighted sometimes at night cruising towards the house of a young lady. Officially, the Crown Prince was chauffeur-driven in a range of European cars. However, the one he liked best was a London cab similar to the landau favoured by his grandmother Queen Sālote. In this vehicle, the tall gentleman could wear his top hat inside without hitting the roof; and, of course, he could also accommodate an important accoutrement of his uniform, namely his ceremonial sword!

Being Commander-in-Chief of the then 72-man Tongan army opened opportunities for HRH to develop his passion for smart uniforms and formal wear. Before he became portly, he cut a fine figure in ornate uniforms with a plumed helmet, resplendent with many decorations, sashes, and with his monocle in place. Dressed in his favoured Edwardian grey suit with tails, he spent hours of practice before the mirror trying to drop his monocle, released with a surprised look, to fall into his top handkerchief pocket. He demonstrated this trick to me in private.

One of the most important occasions was the midnight reception on New Year's Eve when the King and Queen received visitors at the Palace and the Police Band played in the garden rotunda. The glamorous HRH in dress uniform easily outshone the military officers who included the sons of nobles of the realm.

On one such occasion, I witnessed him surreptitiously lacing the huge bowl of the usually non-alcoholic tropical fruit punch preferred by teetotallers with bottles of vodka. Many staid European ladies, including matronly missionary wives, dressed in formal gowns, became disoriented and were seen tottering off into the bushes, whilst the band played on and HRH watched gleefully.

This was before Tonga had a navy. As explained in an earlier chapter, my Letter of Marque was never issued and finally two de Havilland patrol boats turned up to become the first vessels of the new Royal Tongan Navy. Amongst other things, this provided HRH the chance to order an admiral's white uniform modelled on the German style with a Kaiser-type gold-decorated cap as opposed to his Kaiser-type helmet that he used for Army parades.

With Tupouto'a at a Palace Garden Party, June 1971

At the bar of the Nuku'alofa Club, HRH claimed the 40-foot long aluminium patrol boats would reach a speed of 20 knots. I challenged this claim. After all, with a crew of overweight Tongan army personnel in hobnail boots (no navy crews yet), and fuel and ammunition, I thought these overloaded aluminium boats would never reach this speed. HRH proposed a wager with me saying I would give him a case of Johnny Walker whisky if the patrol boat made 20 knots or more and he would give me a case if the boat could not reach 20 knots. I foolishly accepted.

"I get seasick in my bathtub, so we will choose a day when it is mirror calm to stage the sea trial and settle the wager," announced the Crown Prince. So, one morning, I received a message from the Palace Office to meet HRH at the navy depot to where I hastened.

Sure enough, a large black bullet-proof Mercedes with motorbike outriders and sirens blaring pulled up. The Crown Prince emerged in his new complete admiral's uniform sporting white gloves and his monocle.

We sat on the cabin top as the boat gained speed in the calm harbour; but, then, HRH spotted a splatter of bird droppings near where we were sitting and, pointing towards it with his gloved hand, ordered the lieutenant in charge to have it removed.

The lieutenant told the sergeant to get on with it and the sergeant ordered a corporal to remove it, who then instructed a private to get out a bucket with lanyard attached and fetch some seawater.

By this time, we were doing over 15 knots and the heavily booted private secured the lanyard around his wrist and cast the bucket overboard where the force of the sudden drag pulled him over the side.

The boat slowed down and HRH raised his monocle to his eye and looked aft to see the struggling soldier floundering in the sea. HRH then turned to me and said in an offhand manner, "Pita, I suppose we had better go back and recover the bucket."

The soldier was going under water for the third time as the crew poked a boat hook in his face. The bucket was lost and the surviving soldier received a loud and severe reprimand from the lieutenant. Nonetheless, we did reach 20 knots and I had to pay for a very expensive case of Johnny Walker whiskey—and not just Red Label because HRH only drank the more expensive Black Label.

As a young man educated overseas, he did not have much time for the Wesleyan or Methodist Church, which was the official State religious body, whose missionary founders had composed part of the Tongan constitution. Tupouto'a suspected that some of the large collections taken from Tongan believers found their way overseas to other overseas branches of the Church and/or its representatives and their families.

Once a year, the protestant churches organized a big Sunday collection called the "*misinale*", followed by a large feast. At the Sunday church service, each family would send a child forward with a fat envelop to the church steward at a table near the altar. The money would be counted and the amount and the family's name read out to the congregation.

Each family tried to outdo their neighbour's contribution and it was amazing how much was collected from these small poor communities. Families would beg, borrow or 'steal', and even sell their livelihood horses and carts to finance the *misinale*. Enormous generosity and hospitality was a cultural attribute of Tongans.

In his dislike of this custom, Tupouto'a, on one occasion when he was the chairman or guest of honour at a small church on one of his estates, placed a 5-pa'anga (Tongan dollars) note in an envelope, which was announced as the first donation of the day. This caused a huge problem because it would be unthinkable to donate more and outdo the future king.

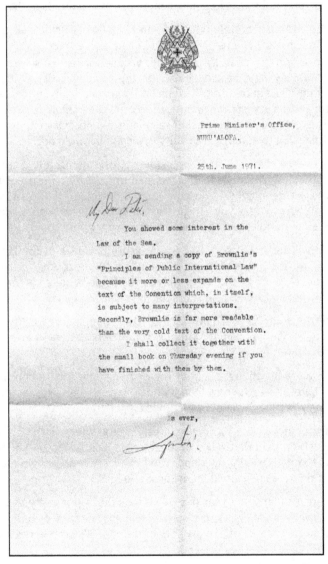

The 'old world' style and charm of a 1971 note from the Crown Prince

The service was tactfully adjourned until a date when the Crown Prince was overseas and then the collection resumed without embarrassment. I suggested to him that he should not alienate himself too much from the Church. He should look more closely at European history to observe that when the Church was strong the king was safe, and when the Church lost power, sometimes the king lost his head. However, privately, we often joked about certain elements of the clergy.

There was an uninhabited island west of Vava'u called Late (pronounced latté) where my crew and I had built a track and erected a trig station[1] on the peak lip of a quiet volcanic lake. This was before GPS technology, and it was built for the Shell Oil Co, which was conducting a seismic survey to see if Tonga had any undersea oil. Tupouto'a was very excited about the possibility of an oil discovery and jokingly exclaimed that his pocket calculator did not have enough zeros in it with which to add up the royalty money that would accrue.

However, I digress. It happened that one of his old Sandhurst friends, the new Sultan of Brunei, wished to send him a present in the form of two tiger cubs. "Trotsky, you know most of the islands in Tonga. Where would you suggest locating the tigers where they are free to roam unmolested?" he asked over the bar at the Nuku'alofa Club.

"I think Late is the spot. There is plenty of water in the lake and wild pigs for the tigers to chase and eat," said I. "But what if they run out of pigs?" he queried. With tongue in cheek I replied, "You could land a few fat Methodist preachers for the tigers to chase."

"No," he said, "they could not run fast enough to give the tigers enough exercise. I suggest landing some thin Catholic priests who could run faster."

Such were his thoughts about the clergy at the time when he was young. Later in life, he developed a healthy regard and respect for the clergy, particularly the learned Orthodox and Catholic priests.

Unfortunately, the Prince's lifestyle together with a family predisposition to diabetes began to affect his health. By 1990 he would bemoan to me, "Trotsky, no longer can I drink six vodka or gin martinis before dinner," as he sipped on the best of wines.

During his many overseas trips, HRH took the opportunity to expand his sartorial wardrobe. For tropical wear he added a colonial white pith helmet with a small solar panel in the top. This powered a small

---

[1]   Triangulation or trigonometrical point—a fixed surveying station, used in geodetic surveying and other surveying projects in its vicinity.

fan inside the top of the helmet. In the sun the fan would start spinning and cool his head. This was a winner.

The old red 1936 model Lockheed, which carried us to Niuafoʻou in 1996

In a San Francisco novelty shop, the Crown Prince came across some shiny black shoes with headlights incorporated in the toe ends. He bought a pair and tested them at night, walking in unlit muddy areas near the Palace. He announced to me that in dry weather they illuminated his path but there was a design fault in as much as he could not see his way forward when the tips of his shoes were covered in mud. He claimed that the shoe ends should have been fitted with headlight wipers for better illumination on rainy nights.

His Majesty Tupou IV encouraged his eldest son to undertake more ceremonial and diplomatic duties, mostly overseas. In about 1972, whilst the cold war still clouded relationships between the West and Russia, the King was considering how he could squeeze some aid money or gifts from the USA, which had shown little interest in Tonga after World War II other than supply US Peace Corps volunteers to the Kingdom. In adroit diplomatic style, HM invited the Soviet ambassador stationed in Wellington to visit some of the islands of Tonga.

Following the visit, the King and the ambassador jointly announced that Russia would build a fishing port facility in the northern harbour of Vavaʻu. Western observers immediately translated the fishing port facility to mean a Soviet naval base. The King sat back and waited for the Yanks to make a counter offer. Nothing happened other than that NZ and Australia took fright and offered more aid to Tonga.

Not really wanting the Russians at all, the King had to think of a way out of the problem because the US were ignoring the Russian bait, so to speak. Adroitly, the dust was blown off an old 99-year Treaty of Friendship entered into with the German Empire signed by Tupou I and the Kaiser of the day, which was soon to expire. Apparently, a clause in the Treaty prohibited Tonga from entering into any adverse arrangements with the enemies of Germany during the lifetime of the Treaty. When he next met the Russian ambassador, Tupou IV was able to say, "My dear ambassador, unfortunately we have just found a clause in an old Treaty which precludes us from entering into the proposed arrangement with the Soviet Union."

Meanwhile, the Crown Prince was dispatched to Germany to negotiate the renewal of the German Treaty. My very good friend, Inoke Faletau (later installed as the matapule 'Akau'ola) who was the Tongan High Commissioner in London, accompanied the Crown Prince to Germany. Inoke later recounted to me in detail that the German media followed and reported every move of the Crown Prince, resplendent in his spectacular old-style German uniforms with matching plumed helmets. To think that a small kingdom in the faraway Pacific should remember, recognize and honour the grand old days of the German Empire aroused the latent emotions of the patriotic German public, especially their politicians.

His first duty was to lay a wreath at the tomb of Kaiser Wilhelm II, Emperor of Germany in 1875 at the time of sealing the Treaty of Friendship with the Kingdom of Tonga. The TV cameras focused on the young, tall and handsome Crown Prince as he laid his wreath and saluted the tomb while the military brass band played nostalgic German hymns and marches. Old German generals present became emotional with tears rolling down their old sabre-scarred cheeks. The visit was enormously successful.

An emotional Germany drowned Tonga with various forms of assistance while Tonga hosted many official and unofficial visitors from Germany. Soon Germany donated a new inter-island ferry and a new-built freighter to the Kingdom and set up a subsidized shipping service for Tonga and Samoa, albeit in competition with the Warner Pacific Line.

A well-equipped technical college with German teachers and administrators followed. These and many more developments unfolded as the bilateral relationship was further enhanced. So, in retrospect, the initial overture to the Soviets opened an avenue for a more beneficial arrangement.

HRH and I at an island party for German naval officers who visited Tonga on a German sail training ship in May 1978

Like Their Majesties, HRH was also an accomplished musician and played a variety of instruments including his favourite, the piano. In our house near the Palace we had one of the two upright pianos in the Kingdom that were kept in tune by the owner of the other good piano, namely the Chief Justice who had other skills in addition to his legal duties. Unless a piano had a solid sounding board and iron frame, it could not be kept in tune for long in the humid climate, which warped many timber objects.

HRH loved playing and listening to classical jazz music. At about 3 am on some occasions, there would be a tapping on our front door and one of his minders would respectfully announce that Tupouto'a wished to practice on our tuned piano. Knowing it would be a long session, I would stagger up, get dressed, send a houseboy out to kill a small pig and take it to the bakery to roast for the Prince's breakfast. Then, reaching for a bottle of Chivas Regal, I would greet HRH at the door. After some hours of pouring his drinks and listening to jazz, which frankly, I do not appreciate, I ventured to say, "Your Highness, I know you are an excellent pianist, but why do you have to practice so long into the early hours of the morning?"

"Well, you see Trotsky, after the revolution I am going to get a job as a nightclub entertainer, so I must keep up my practice," he replied; after which I dropped such unseemly questions.

The call for democracy was becoming more strident in some quarters but, overall, the Tongans respected the royal family who, unfortunately, were perceived by some, to live in isolation from their subjects. There were always plenty of people grovelling before them seeking favours and it was hard to sort the good intentions of some people from the self-seeking greedy ambitions of others.

In my opinion, a great mentor in Tupouto'a's life was Humphrey Arthington-Davy who became Her Britannic Majesty's High Commissioner and Consul to Tonga in 1973. He hailed from the Indian Army, and had served as an officer and diplomat in many outposts of the shrinking British Empire. Humphrey's jaw had been partially shot away by a sniper in Burma and he had a somewhat distorted but jovial look about him. He was the typical English bachelor with ageing parents living somewhere in the English countryside. His informal and affable manner was augmented by his elegant but casual style of attire.

The dress code at most functions at the British residency was "Aloha"—Hawaiian shirts for the gentlemen and colourful "*muumuus*" (Hawaiian long dresses) for women. This was a big change from Humphrey's stuffy predecessors.

During the time when Tonga was a British protectorate, the residing British High Commissioner had quite an influence in Tongan Foreign affairs. Even after complete independence, the Tongans generally heeded British advice and were recipients of sensible British aid projects. After all, the Brits had been doing this sort of thing for centuries as their empire expanded. The local princes of many colonies and protectorates were offered the best English education. Most developed into Anglophiles and admired many of the British traits. Tupouto'a was amongst them and had school and university friends in the UK with other royals including the very wealthy young Sultan of Brunei. HRH confided what he saw as English peculiarities to me: "Trotsky, why do the Brits send their children to cold boarding schools in Scotland to live a life of hardship, whilst they keep their dogs at home, well fed and resting in front of warm fires with the family?"

Tupouto'a felt at home with Humphrey and, I suspect, received some wise advice, whilst outwardly projecting the attitude of a laidback eccentric playboy, influenced by his mixing with other young royals and nobles. When Humphrey retired after many years of service, he remained in Tonga where he died. One of Tupouto'a's most treasured gifts was a small decorated wooden deed box that Humphrey bequeathed to him.

Back in the 1970s, the King and Queen wanted to get Tupouto'a married off as soon as possible but the young prince objected to being organised by the family. All royal marriages in Tonga are arranged. Under Tongan royal protocol and tradition, a member of the royal family may only marry members of Tongan nobility; in other words, no commoners allowed.

Through the eyes of Tongan males, to be big is to be beautiful. Of course many robust daughters of pushy nobles were offered, but HRH was not interested. Under pressure, he finally agreed—much to the delight of both sets of parents—to pursue Nanasi Vaea, the daughter of Noble Vaea who held a high position in government as a minister of the Crown.

Meanwhile a suitable wedding present had to be found befitting a prince. What do you give a prince who appeared to have everything? It had to be something grand, not another silver teapot. After much thought I decided to buy the wedded couple a boudoir grand piano—in other words, a baby grand piano which cost us $A8,000 in Sydney. It was shipped to Tonga where it lay in the locked customs wharf shed for months whilst Tupouto'a further delayed the wedding. I was not willing to pay duty on it or arrange delivery until close to the wedding day.

However, Tupouto'a was procrastinating and delaying any announcements. Then there was a hurricane, which swept away the contents of the wharf warehouse. The baby grand floated around in seawater, which wrecked all its interior, while the exterior polished shell survived.

Finally, in a face saving manoeuver, it was announced that Nanasi was going to marry the youngest brother of Tupouto'a; and, so, HRH was off the hook while both families were satisfied.

The wrecked piano was finally delivered to the Palace where it was used for display purposes only. Tupouto'a never married. Thus, as it turned out, Nanasi became the Queen anyway upon the death of Tupouto'a.

As HRH grew older, he became more conservative and some of the earlier mischief faded. HRH served as Minister for Foreign Affairs from 1979 to 1998 when he retired from government service. He remained mostly a good investor and expanded his business interests. Some said he used his position to negotiate favourable deals; but I think foreigners also encouraged him to take up part ownership in local activities with a view to gaining an entry into Tongan-based enterprises. Not all his ideas were successful. I was appointed a director of Tonga Oil, a government owned company, which aimed to buy fuels on the spot market, but it never really got going.

When the French ceased exploding underwater atomic devices at Mururoa Atoll, they had a surplus coastal fuel tanker, which they gave to the Tonga Navy in appreciation of HRH's neutrality in not criticizing their unpopular atomic experiment in the Pacific. Tonga Oil was supposed to use the tanker but it was not a viable vessel for long distances.

Mele Vikatolia Faletau, the Oxford educated eldest daughter of 'Evelini and Inoke Faletau had the privilege of serving HRH when he was Minister for Foreign Affairs and Defence and, later, as his personal secretary. She felt HRH was hurt when his father and sister wanted to change and recognize mainland China.

Tupouto'a was always loyal to his closest friends, even though he often abused us. Although his father, the king, and his sister could see commercial benefits in recognizing what had now become the People's Republic of China, Tupouto'a was reluctant to give up the close association with Republic of China—now relocated to Taiwan. Tonga could not recognize both. Amongst his many close but abused friends was Sosefo Ramanlal (Indian father, Tongan mother) whom HRH called a "curry muncher" and worse.

HRH did not enjoy living in the Palace and built a large villa along the lines of a large Italian palazzo. It was equipped with an elaborate commercial-size kitchen. One of his other friends was Masa, a Japanese fisherman and excellent cook. Masa had come to Tonga as a Japanese aid volunteer to operate a long line fishing boat provided by Japan as aid to Tonga. Masa decided to stay in Tonga and could speak better Tongan than I could. He used to cook special dishes for HRH.

Early one morning, close to arriving at Nuku'alofa, I caught a rather nice yellow fin tuna which I sent up to the villa for HRH. Later in the day, I was summonsed to be at the Villa for dinner soon after sunset because Masa was preparing the large very fresh fish. Sitting around the stainless steel kitchen with HRH, Masa tried to explain the various dishes, soups, sashimi, sushi and barbecued steaks he was making from the tuna.

Tupouto'a commented, "Masa, speak to me in Tongan; your English is awful."

To change the subject I said, "Your Highness, you know this meal in Tokyo would cost us $US1,000 per head."

To this he replied, "If first you could get it and secondly as fresh as this," which made me happy.

Masa eventually graduated to become the future ceremonial head taster for Tupou V, especially at Kava functions where traditionally the taster takes the first drink—which may have been poisoned—before the King imbibes. This position was traditionally granted to a high-ranking foreigner.

HRH nicknamed his hard working secretary "Miss Money Penny". She—Mele Vikatolia—travelled all over the world with HRH, and recalls many amusing and colourful events. Amongst other duties, she handled the movement of his large number of bags, arranged tickets and dealt with his tailors, car drivers and uniformed staff and party and function arrangements, decorations and even fancy dress fittings.

Money Penny recalls one safari into Mongolia, when Tupouto'a's baggage occupied one full tent. He had ordered her to obtain a king size blow up mattress which turned out to be too big to fit in his single tent. She recalls the staff and her struggling to accommodate it. On the following page is a photo of the Crown Prince in pith helmet and desert boots in the Mongolian desert.

The nickname for all his Asian interpreters was "Cherry Blossom". Near the border of Mongolia and China, HRH announced that he was tired of the greasy lamb food of the desert and would take Money Penny and Cherry Blossom to dinner at a Chinese restaurant in the evening.

Arriving by car, he studied the menu and asked Cherry Blossom if she would like anything special. Of course, Cherry Blossom meekly said no and that she would enjoy anything His Highness would choose.

Then he asked the same question of Money Penny, to which she respectfully replied, that she would leave the selection to his superior taste. After further study of the menu he announced, "Then tonight we will have something different."

With a glint in his eye, he ordered the waiter to show them the selection of snakes on offer. The waiters produced the live snakes squirming in clear plastic bags and the Crown Prince selected one, which was killed in the kitchen.

Dressed for the Mongolian Desert: HRH, Tupou Kaho and Annie Kaneshiro

This was presented cooked in various ways in various dishes culminating with a glass of snake blood mixed with alcohol. The two ladies were horrified. Cherry Blossom said she was not really hungry, and asked if her portion could be put in a bag to take home. Money Penny claimed a sudden illness and excused herself from the sight. Tupouto'a munched away happily.

On another occasion in Egypt, Mele, alias Money Penny, had to fit out the group with Egyptian fancy dress and a fez hat for each male. This was for a party. See the photograph on the facing page.

Mele (Miss Money Penny) had been to school with my daughters who kept in contact through life. After graduating from Oxford University, she married Mailifihi, a noble and nephew of Tupou IV. Unfortunately, this did not last. After their divorce, her husband died early in life, but her eldest son now carries the title HSH Prince Tu'ipelehake.

10. The eccentric Crown Prince

Egyptian fancy dress party on board Abercrombie and Kent

It is now clear to the reader that the Crown Prince was obsessed with clothes and uniforms and suffered from what I call the peacock syndrome. He could outshine the crown heads of Europe, sultans, maharajahs and lesser dignitaries whether in uniform or Edwardian morning coat. Money Penny and, I think, he must have been very proud of the article published in the British Gentleman's Gazette about the British Royal wedding in London in 2011, which said, "One of the most interesting outfits was worn by the King of Tonga. He pulled off a mid-grey 6 x 2 frock coat with vibrant blue lining and partial silk facings on the lapels, matching trousers, black shoes/boots and grey spats. It's an exceptional combination to say the least."

As he grew older, his health deteriorated but it did not diminish his zest for life. The Australian government gave two bigger and better patrol boats to the Tongan Navy as aid, but there was little money to buy fuel for regular surveillance voyages, so HRH suggested to Australia that they should also provide a spotter plane, which could be sent out to patrol the Tongan waters. The Australians agreed in principle.

Tupouto'a thought a small seaplane would be most suitable and we discussed the type. I liked a small plane with floats, which was made in Miami and came in a crate to be assembled. HRH did not like the idea of assembling it in Tonga because he had little confidence in his local mechanics. He said that there would be too many washers, screws and nuts left over when the assembly was completed.

Eventually, in 1996, HRH acquired a very old twin engine plane, together with the services of a dare-devil American pilot who had survived a few crashes and had a stainless steel plate in his head. I think it was a Lockheed Electra 10 built about 1935 capable of carrying up to ten normal size passengers or five Tongans. It was in this type of plane that Amelia Earhart disappeared. It was also the same sort of private plane favoured by old film stars of the 1930s and 40s. The advantage was that it ran on regular petrol and not aviation gas. You could fill up at any petrol service station.

Before Tupouto'a retired from government, one of our last jaunts together in 1996 was, for me, a terrifying flight in this old aircraft to Niuafo'ou which was one of the northern most islands in Tonga. We regularly carried passengers and cargo there, usually on our way to and from Samoa. The island had a hot and smouldering volcanic crater and was "steep to" without a harbour. It was a difficult place to land from the sea but a small airstrip had been built.

The island had been evacuated completely in 1936 during a large eruption. After World War II, some of the population returned with Father Callet, an intrepid priest from France. By 1980 this devoted priest of this small remote island was going blind. On a voyage there, I was given a letter by the Bishop in Nuku'alofa to deliver personally into the hands of the Father. It turned out to be a letter dismissing him because of his failing eyesight and ordering him to return to Nuku'alofa with me.

I shall never forget the total island's population weeping at the landing place upon his departure, as he boarded the surfboat in his gown, with all his worldly possessions, a walking stick and a small leather suitcase. Such gratitude, as expressed by his devoted flock, is rarely witnessed. However, it was not to be his last duty in Tonga. His wartime parish in France paid for his cataract surgery, gave him a bell from the ruins of their bombed church and sent him back to Tonga with the bell, where he became a senior member of the Catholic mission. He was placed in charge of building a basilica in Nuku'alofa and served mankind again for many years.

But I divert. The official reason for the flight and stay on Niuafo'ou was to explore how to spend some granted aid money there, and make recommendations to the donors. To undertake this study in depth, HRH decided that he needed to send the army ahead in a landing craft to set up camp, refrigeration for our drinks and a well-equipped field kitchen with gourmet food and a good chef. Petrol for the return flight was added plus a jeep.

A couple of his secretaries went with the advance party. They were chosen for their skill in playing contract bridge and poker. We boarded this old aircraft in Tonga and, much to my amazement, it was lined inside with only plywood which had soaked up petrol and smelt like it would catch fire at any moment. Tupouto'a took up the co-pilot's seat and we were airborne. The pilot and he lit large cigars which added to the fire risk and then Tupouto'a took over the controls and we weaved through the sky, diving sometimes down to see some of the remote islands on the way. Fortunately, the American pilot found the right island and landed on the narrow strip with only a few bumps. To my great relief we had escaped, but I would have felt much happier if HRH had let me return on the landing barge.

The camp by the lake was well chosen; we stayed three days and played bridge every night, sometimes until three in the morning or until the generator broke down. Tupouto'a dealt with the locals in only one day and we enjoyed ourselves for the rest, guarded from local intrusion by the military guards.

Some local delicacies were presented including eggs from a strange bird—a megapode—which laid them in the warm sands of the crater. I found feathers and a cooked chick in mine. Little was done in exploring development projects but when we returned, I wrote a report and gave it to the Government—a summary copy is included as an addendum to this book. I do not think much of the report was adopted but I thought it justified my inclusion in the terrifying joy ride. Luckily, the return flight was made safely, and I thanked HRH for the interesting experience. I think he enjoyed scaring me.

Shore Line Power was one of Tupouto'a's controversial investments. Over the years, the slow revving generators provided by the British to the government, owned by the Power Board in Nuku'alofa, were becoming unreliable because of poor service and shortage of parts. The town was growing and the generators were not coping with the load so consequently the residents suffered many blackouts.

Tupouto'a proposed that the government should privatise the electricity supply and his company Shoreline take over the monopoly of providing electricity. If this had not eventuated, I feel sure the old system would have broken down completely like most underfunded government projects do in most countries; in which case we would all have been left in the dark! The government had little choice, and Tupouto'a and his partners raised considerable international financing and turned the business into a profitable business, albeit with risk. For the first time the banks asked him to personally guarantee the loan that his company took out with which to buy all new generators.

The price of electricity gradually increased and the public increasingly grew unhappy over the years. They soon forgot that they may have been in complete darkness if he had not acted and also forgot that the price of fuel for the generators was also increasing every year. Under much criticism, he eventually sold the service back to the government when it had sufficient funds. Upon becoming King in 2008 he disposed of all his remaining business interests.

Tupouto'a was generally unappreciated, misunderstood and underestimated by the people during his time as Crown Prince. Behind the flamboyant front was a deep thinker with a sharp brain who pulled no punches whilst projecting an air of poise and culture. Although he was to rule a proud parochial people steeped in local tradition and dogma, he himself held international views. As an example, he was recorded as saying during the Fiji racial troubles in 2000, "Many countries have racially-biased land laws and, in Tonga's case, these have been enshrined for so long that they have become hallowed by time, and have undeservedly assumed the quality of religion and cultural truth." Many other wise comments have been recorded.

When I arrived in Tonga, there were only nine elected commoners in the Parliament. By the time of his death, there were 17, which is an indication of his plans for slow steps towards democracy, and to see if democracy would work within a tribally-oriented traditional population, new to global impacts. Perhaps they will not be able to control themselves and become another "basket case" of self-governed countries within the Pacific.

As Tupou V, he was heard to say that democracy was not for the lesser educated and only worked in a sophisticated atmosphere. Unfortunately, he was right: as democracy became obligatory for colonies and tribal countries, those, in turn, bred twisted dictators and bent politicians.

After I left Tonga, his coronation took place in 2008, two years after his father's death. But he only ruled for six years before succumbing to leukaemia in a Hong Kong hospital with his brother and future king at his bedside.

So ended my friendship with the most colourful and eccentric character I have ever met in this last remaining kingdom in the Pacific.

Coronation of HM King George Tupou V

The official portrait of HM King George Tupou V

11
Start of Warner
Pacific Line

11
Start of Warner Pacific Line

The chapters covering the rise and fall of Warner Pacific Line have been the most difficult for me to write; the lesson being that one should never chew off more than one can digest. It started small, grew successfully, peaked and then struggled; partly because I was too ambitious, partly because I expected my Tongan officers to be more careful, and partly because the commercial pirates of the Pacific sucked me in and spat me out.

The embryo idea to launch a cargo service named Warner Pacific Line (WPL) was first conceived when my fishing boats started to carry deck passengers, odd bits of cargo, live animals and the mail from island to island whilst we were *en route* to and from our fishing grounds. These diversions included the odd charter to carry officials and missionaries, plus one charter to carry the King of Tonga, Tupou IV, to claim a new island thrust up by volcanic activity near Hunga Tonga, 40 miles northwest of Nuku'alofa. As the sea was too rough to land a boat on the patch of scoria, His Majesty expressed his desire to take a sample of the island home, whereupon about six young enthusiastic followers in his entourage leapt into the sea and swam across before diving down to recover handfuls of volcanic ash. Upon returning, I asked one of the divers what it was like under the surface. He replied, "Very hot and noisy with loud rumblings."

All these side issues distracted me from fishing. Among these diversions was a hearse service carrying dead bodies to their home islands for burial. People emigrated to the capital Nuku'alofa from outer islands for many reasons. Some eventually died in Nuku'alofa and the health law required that burials must occur within 24 hours unless the body was embalmed. Otherwise, they get smelly in the tropics. Tradition called for the mourners to bury their dead relative on the island where he or she was born.

People seemed to die between 2 am and 3 am in Nuku'alofa; and my sleep was often disturbed at about 4 am by some weeping mourner requesting a charter of one of my fishing vessels to carry the body and mourners to an island. Mostly they pleaded no money, but having been exposed before to this risk, I always sent the mourner off to find money and went back to bed. Before dawn, I would be woken again and would have to count coins and notes of many denominations, issued by many countries, to make up the value of the charter. Often the crew, mourners and body were already on board before I had finished counting. Accompanied by much hymn singing, we would depart.

On this occasion, the body was laid out in the workboat carried on deck. We arrived at our destination after dark and the small workboat with some mourners and the body was hoisted over the side and paddled ashore to an avenue of palm torches formed in the shallow water between wading, waiting, weeping and singing relatives. They lifted my workboat together with the body and disappeared inland to the cemetery in the dark. Hastily, I sent a crewmember ashore to make sure my boat was not buried with the body.

In the 1970s, a small funeral lasted five days and important ones much longer until the chief mourner was bankrupt. Tradition dictated that the chief mourner provides food and tea to a large throng of mourners—and anybody else who turned up—for as many days as possible until all funds were exhausted. We did not stay long at these events and sailed on the next sunrise. Tongan funerals are an emotional affair and these island burials will remain in my memory for ever.

Meanwhile three years (1968–1972) of intensive fishing activities was not producing enough protein to satisfy the demand for all types of fish in Nuku'alofa. We exported the crayfish tails and sold everything else locally. The Union Shipping company discharged other forms of refrigerated protein on the monthly call to Nuku'alofa and Vava'u. Lamb flaps, sometimes salted down, were most popular and cheapest, but did not last very long. I had freezers on my barges and in some of the fishing boats.

After lengthening MV *Ata* to 80 feet in 1972, I planned a trial voyage from Tonga to the South Island of New Zealand carrying bananas south and buying a cargo of frozen lamb flaps for the return voyage to Tonga. A few trial voyages between fishing activities proved successful, but MV *Ata* was too small to carry the quantity of cargo demanded. The voyage was too far to be economically viable for the small vessel. So I started searching anywhere in the world for a smallish refrigerated cargo vessel to meet my specifications.

MV *Frysna*

MV *Frysna* approaching Tafahi Island

Because of earlier experience with Scandinavian ships, I narrowed the search down to Norway, Sweden and Holland where suitable second-hand vessels could be found. Vessels that have traded in the North Sea and Baltic have rusted less than those in the tropics and hence have a longer life.

Eventually I found the MV *Frysna*, 487 tons in deadweight tonnage (dwt[1]), built in France in 1964. It was a fully refrigerated vessel at a price of $US220,000 and located in Norway.

In January 1973, I arranged a loan of $US200,000 from the Nordic Bank, London office. Then, I went to the Tongan treasury where I kept my traders deposit account and asked for a treasury cheque for $US20,000. I was told the Kingdom did not have $US20,000 in their US bank account, but there was a cruise liner due in a few days and Treasury expected that passengers would leave more than $20,000 in notes which local traders would cash in at the Treasury soon after the ship departed. So I agreed to take $US20,000 in cash with me on the flight to London where the sale was to be concluded at the Nordic Bank.

The day before I flew out of Tonga, I sent my clerk to the Treasury to collect the cash, and he returned with a small suitcase full of dirty used $1, $5 and $10 US currency notes, which never left my side on the long flight to London. It was a bit awkward going to the small toilets on the plane with a suitcase.

The settlement at the bank was due on a Monday, but I arrived on a weekend with all this cash and nowhere to hide it. Fortunately, one of my best friends, Inoke Faletau (later Hon 'Akau'ola) was Tongan High Commissioner in London and had a safe at his home where we deposited the cash, much to my relief.

On Monday morning, I arrived at the boardroom of the bank and emptied all the notes on the table. I do not think the bank directors had seen real cash money before, and they sent it off to some minions to count. Meanwhile they gave me a handwritten receipt for a suitcase alleged to contain $US20,000. The settlement went according to plan and I flew out to Bergen to meet the ship and the Tongan crew, newly arrived in the winter snow.

---

[1] dwt is not the weight of the empty ship but the total weight of what a ship can carry without riding dangerously low in the water (i.e., so that her Plimsoll line is at water level), including cargo, fuel, fresh water, ballast water, provisions, passengers, and crew.

MV *Kemphaan*

My small crew of seven Tongans whom I had selected from the fishing boats in Ha'apai took their first flight in a plane, via New York to Bergen, Norway and arrived in their traditional tropical clothing, wearing sandals in the snow. Before I arrived, the Norwegian ships agent soon had them fitted out in warm clothes and showed them how the heating worked in the ship's accommodation. Before leaving Tonga, I had advised them to bring some handicraft, especially baskets, as gifts for the Norwegians. Upon arrival, the agent took me to the snow-covered ship, where loud music and steam issued from within. I found a big party in swing with scantily clad blond Norwegian girls cavorting with the young Tongan crew.

"You were right," said Filipe Panuve, "one basket gets you one girl!"

We sailed around to Stockholm to load a cargo of frozen pig carcasses for Japan through waters that I had known in my youth. I left the ship in Stockholm in the hands of a Norwegian skipper and engineer whom I had engaged for the delivery voyage to Tonga via the Panama Canal and Japan. No cargo could be found from Japan to Tonga so the first real ship of WP Line sailed empty from Japan to start its first voyage south with bananas from Tonga to New Zealand.

MV *Frysna* was a success but, at only 487 tons, still could not keep up with the growing demand for frozen cargo from New Zealand to Tonga and onwards to the two Samoas. Between islands, we still carried deck passengers and deck cargo in what I called the three "P" deck cargo made up of people, pigs and perishables.

So, I started looking for an additional freezer ship and luckily found one in Cairns, Australia. It was a small Dutch freezer vessel built in 1959, slightly larger than MV *Frysna* at 560 dwt tons. It had been running food provisions from Cairns during the construction of a big copper mine at Bougainville. Now, the construction was finished and the MV *Kemphaan* was for sale. Her hull was sound but the refrigeration was an old-fashioned ammonia system, which was leaky and dangerous.

I bought MV *Kemphaan* in Cairns for $160,000 in late 1973. I skippered it myself for four months in early 1974, during which time we executed a charter carrying frozen prawns from trawlers in the Gulf of Carpentaria through Torres Strait and down to Cairns. It was a very wet season with several severe tropical storms. I remember dodging around many deep cyclonic eyes, foul winds, strong currents and plenty of reefs to rendezvous with the trawlers in poor visibility in the rain.

Before mid-1974, MV *Kemphaan* had joined the Warner Pacific Line service between New Zealand and Tonga and Samoa. The refrigeration had a habit of breaking down on the way to the South Island of New Zealand with bananas on board. Unless held in air changing refrigeration, a few ripening bananas can give off a noxious gas, which generates more heat and ripens all the remaining cargo. Quick decisions have to be made. On one occasion during a major refrigeration failure, I remember radioing the consignee for instructions to divert or even jettison the cargo. Reply was, "Open all the hatches and full speed to Timaru." This worked and the ripening bananas were successfully discharged.

Nonetheless, *Kemphaan* served us well until its last fateful voyage in June 1978, when it departed Timaru with a full cargo of lamb flaps heading north. During the first night at sea off Lyttleton about 20 miles out to sea, a fire started in the engine room. We think it was caused by a fractured fuel line spraying oil over the hot exhaust manifold. The engine room and the after accommodation were soon well ablaze. The awakened survivors scuttled forward without time to send any distress signals. To their horror, one of the crew did not make it and died in the inferno. This was Sami Totau (brother of Mano Totau). Another, Viliami, the electrician, was seriously burned and later died in hospital.

Daylight came over the burning wreck with the survivors huddling in the bow of the ship. The lifeboats and rafts were burnt, but an aluminum workboat and solid raft were on deck. The workboat was launched, and two of the crew paddled westward towards land, which was not visible. The exhausted pair made landfall well after dark, beached and found a farmhouse to raise the alarm.

A tug was dispatched from Lyttelton and found the skipper and surviving crew on the solid raft, still made fast to the bow of the burning hull. The tug then turned its fire hose onto the burning hull, but by then the fire had worked its way forward to the frozen lamb flaps in the hold. Full of fat, the lamb flaps were creating a giant barbecue, so the tug captain abandoned the firefighting exercise, attached a towrope to the bow and towed the burning wreck into the outer harbour at Lyttelton. Here he grounded the wreck on a mud bank and poured water into the hull until it was submerged and the fire extinguished.

Meanwhile I had boarded a plane from Tonga with the young wife of Viliami, and arrived in Lyttelton to help the crew and make necessary arrangements. The Lyttelton harbour master confronted me and told me to remove my wreck from his harbour. I told him, "You put it there, so you can remove it." So, before the cargo became completely rotten, the hull was pumped dry, refloated and towed well out to sea, where the New Zealand Air Force used it for bombing practice. After many bombing runs, it finally sank to a watery grave.

From then on in the small WP Line fleet, there was always one ship named MV *Vili* and one named MV *Sami*, in memory of the two brave young men lost on MV *Kemphaan*. Eventually there were two ships named *Sami I* and *Sami II*.

MV *Sami*

MV *Sami* in Sydney 1980

We returned to Tonga. After the funerals had been held and the underwriters had paid out my claim for total loss, I started searching for a replacement vessel. In late 1974 I bought an old vessel named MV *Capitaine Cook* from the French company, Sofrana Line. It had been trading for some years between Noumea and Wallis and Futuna Islands. At 1,300 tons, it had a bigger carrying capacity than the two freezer ships, with a large general cargo hold and a small freezer hold forward. Already 28 years old and due for a very expensive special survey when reaching 32 years of age, I knew I would only enjoy four years of service out of her; but she was a cheap buy with little delivery expense.

A "*modus operandi*" was developing, caused by a shortage of capital, to buy or charter old ships of about 20 years of age and try to run them until they were due for their very expensive special survey at around 32 years of age. Most modern ships' owners write off and sell their ships at about 20 years of age as repair costs increase. So, having acquired a ship, changed flag, and fully manned it with a Tongan crew, I would try to do as much maintenance as possible in Tonga where it was cheaper than in New Zealand and Australia.

Crew salaries were set by the South Pacific Bureau for Economic Cooperation. For example, in 1974 an Ordinary Seaman earned $A126 per month and electricians $A161, plus what they could make from smuggling.

MV *Sami* could lift one full container

MVs *Frysna* and *Vili* together at Queen Sālote Wharf, Nuku'alofa

To minimize costs further, I would run a ship at a lower cruising speed than designed, for example, reducing the cruising revs from 1,200 rpm to say 900 rpm. This saved a lot of wear and tear on the main engines and saved fuel albeit slowing down each voyage. Thus, the daily running costs of WP Line were lower than younger European manned and operated vessels. Most of WP Line vessels were in a class with the French survey society Bureau Veritas.

The MV *Capitaine Cook* ran well and we carried Tupou IV, the King of Tonga, to witness another volcanic eruption on a reef just south of Late Island which had formed a temporary sandy cay. We approached cautiously with echo sounder charting the rising sea floor. Before this island disappeared, a group of us including one of the King's nobles landed in a lifeboat and planted the Tongan flag.

In September 1980, just before MV *Capitaine Cook* was due for its expensive special survey, we loaded a cargo of drummed tallow for a small Chinese port, delivered the cargo and returned to Hong Kong where I had pre-sold the ship to a nice old Chinaman who specialised in this type of deal. He paid me scrap value. I asked him where he would scrap the vessel, because I thought the time and cost of undertaking a thorough survey of such an old vessel would be unviable anywhere.

"No," he replied, "I will sail it to the land of gifts, to Bangkok where I know a very friendly Bureau Veritas surveyor who will pass it for special survey." He was smarter than I was and sent me a telegram some weeks later to say, "Survey passed stop loaded full cargo rice stop now en route Bahrain." The crew and I flew back to Tonga from Hong Kong.

From 1945 to about 1990, there were many small independent shipping companies operating in the international waters of the free Pacific. They carried all types of cargoes and some passengers before the days of container ships. Besides the French Sofrana Line, which grew large, there was another colourful owner/captain operating between Sydney and Noumea, as well as Reef Shipping, which sailed between New Zealand and Fiji, Silk and Boyd in the Cook Islands and the so-called Cook Island National Line, which was operated by some locals. All Lines issued their own bills of lading to shippers who paid their freight. The ship owners knew that whoever held the original bill of lading owned the cargo. Cargo was not released on delivery unless the original bill of lading was produced. The back of the bill of lading set out the conditions of carriage in fine print. The conditions were based on old Admiralty laws and/or Carriage of Goods Acts.

Wise shippers insured their cargoes with cargo underwriters knowing that the carrier's liability was limited. Likewise, ship owners joined Protection and Indemnity insurance clubs to protect them against (amongst other things) any major claims made by cargo owners or underwriters. Cargo owners made all sorts of claims against carriers. Many carriers employed a claims clerk to sort out these claims. An anonymous wag in a shipping office wrote the poem below, which summarized the way all Pacific Island shipping companies dodged liability. Of course, the poem was never shown to clients.

Shipowner's Liability

It is much to be regretted
That your goods are slightly wetted,
But our lack of liability is plain,
for our latest bill of lading,
which is proof against evading,
bears exception for sea-water, rust and rain,
also sweat contamination,
fire and all depreciation,
that we've ever seen or heard of on a ship.
And our due examination,
which we made at destination,

shows your cargo much improved by the trip.
Furthermore, the protest shows
that the master blew his nose,
and the hatches were demolished by the gale.
Oh, we'll all stick together
to prove it's a heavy weather,
for we've got the cargo-owner by the tail.
So reserving all defences,
Alibis and false pretences,
We suggest that your underwriter man,
Is the guy that's out of luck.
We always pass the buck,
Yes—we always duck the issue if we can.
This of course is grief sincere,
And we almost weep to hear,
you are claiming for your cargo wet by rain,
it really is a crime
that you are wasting all your time,
For our bill of lading clauses make it plain
that from ullage, rust or seepage,
water sweat, or just plain leakage,
Act of God, restraint of Princes, theft or war,
loss, damage or detention,
Lock out, strike or circumvention,
blockade, interdict or lost twixt ship and shore,
quarantine or heavy weather,
fog or rain, or both together.
We're protected from all these and many more
and it's very plain to see
that our liability,
as regards to your claim is absolutely nil.
So try your underwriter,
he's a friendly sort of blighter,
and is pretty sure to grin and foot the bill.

Other than our regular liner service from NZ and sometimes
Australia to Tonga and Samoa, we took an odd charter to strange
places. Amongst these was the drummed inedible tallow we
transported from NZ to China. Because our ships were small and
shallow-drafted we could navigate the many small, Chinese rivers
before China developed deep-water ports. Sailing north, we always left
the Philippines to port because we had no desire to sail through the
pirate-infested waters of the South China Sea. This was an unruly sea,
which had been so for many centuries. Our slow steaming ships were

easy targets. The New Zealanders exported so-called "inedible" tallow in drums as well as in specially heated Russian tankers to China to be made into candles and soap, but it is my belief most of it was used as dripping in everyday cooking.

Other interesting voyages were to Fanning and Christmas Islands in the Pacific close to the equator to load copra for Burns Philp who owned Fanning Island at the time. The Line Islands, as they are called, are most interesting with a huge lagoon at Christmas Island about 8 miles in diameter, brightly coloured by red brine shrimps. It is all part of the Republic of Kiribati now, but in those days they were British colonies. Later in 1985, charter voyages from Apia to the Tokelau Islands were undertaken on behalf of the New Zealand Government who administered these remote places.

Two other successful small ships of the line were the Dutch built MVs *Aidan* and *Josephine*. An old and crafty Dutch owner named Mr Dammers had slowly built up a fleet of 11 of these sister ships, 1,000 dwt tons each, to trade in the Caribbean. They were all registered in Curacao, which was some sort of Dutch tax haven. Eventually I bought two of these handy and cheap-to-operate vessels, which had general cargo and freezer capacity. The first was MV *Aidan* built in 1962. This was bought in 1975 and served well. The MV *Josephine*, which I renamed MV *Sami* was bought in the early 1980s. All ships were reflagged and registered in Nuku'alofa.

MV *Aidan*

MVs *Frysna* and *Aidan* together

Before the loss of the *Kemphaan* in 1978, I had never changed the name of any acquired vessel. Nautical superstition said it was bad luck to change the name of a ship or to sail from any port on Friday 13th. In fact, I had once worked for one old Norwegian owner who would not get out of bed on a Friday the 13th and issued a directive to all his captains not to set sail on that date. However, because I wished to remember the two brave lost sailors on the *Kemphaan*, I took the step to rename the MV *Josephine* as MV *Sami* when first I bought it, and later renamed the MV *Nogi* as MV *Vili*. Thereafter I rejected the superstition and renamed other ships.

All of these early small ships made money—not huge profits because they did not carry huge cargoes, but they serviced small communities well and gave me a thrill to be of service in a small way. Satisfaction in serving mankind was more my aim rather than making obscene amounts of money. I enjoyed a great sense of fulfilment from pioneering new routes and adopting novel operational techniques. However, times were changing. More expensive container ships were making inroads into Pacific Island trades. Ships were getting bigger but fewer in number so island communities received less frequent visits from larger ships. In the days of trading schooners, islanders could travel and ship small quantities of cargo frequently, but this was changing. Economy of scale was now the buzz phrase in business. To stay in any trade, one had to do things in a bigger way to survive or be driven out by bigger operators with deeper pockets.

When one becomes moderately successful in business, everybody wants to lend you money or become your agent, partner, or hire (charter) you ships and equipment. When times are tough, nobody wants to know you. Pushed to expand, my appetite for power grew to a point that my stomach had difficulties in digesting the intake.

Warner Pacific Line Office—Nuku'alofa

12
The slippery slope

12
The slippery slope

A good decision that turned out bad was when Warner Pacific Line bought its second old ship from Sofrana Unilines in 1982. We renamed it MV *Tasi*, which means "one" in the Samoan language but was also the name of the son of the Hon. Fakafonua, my local noble in Tonga.

It was a Norwegian built ship of 2,350 dwt tons with a large cubic capacity, high sides and three decks. Designed for pallet carrying, it had originally been a side loader but the side doors had been welded closed. Sofrana had installed a small out-of-class freezer in one of the lower holds. It had a strange propulsion arrangement with two diesel motors connected to one propeller shaft via a complex gearbox including some very big gear wheels. It could run on one engine only. It serviced the New Zealand/Tonga/Samoa trade well. Frequently it sailed south to Nelson to load cement from the Golden Bay Cement Company as a base cargo before proceeding to Onehunga or Auckland to load general and freezer cargo.

MV *Tasi*

MV *Tasi* in Sydney 1982

On one voyage northbound, MV *Tasi* had taken on nearly a full load of palletized bagged cement on three decks before proceeding out across Cook Strait into a winter storm. The chief officer had failed to prop and lash the cargo securely; so, when the ship was dumped by one of the big beam seas, the cargo shifted. MV *Tasi* took on an extreme list to port as the cargo finally stacked into the lee side of the holds.

A radio Mayday distress signal brought two ships to the scene, but the mature, brave and stubborn Captain Polonga refused to abandon the ship and would not allow any of the crew to try to launch life rafts, although many wanted to. The ship had such a list that the port lifeboat was almost in the water while the starboard one could not be launched. Expecting it to sink at any moment the two rescue ships accompanied the listing ship during the stormy night. Using one of the two main engines, MV *Tasi* maneuvered towards Nelson, like a large storm-driven yacht with lee deck well awash.

MV *Tasi* listing to port

MV *Tasi*—like a large storm-driven yacht with lee deck well awash

Had I known what insurance problems would arise, I would have gladly ordered the captain to abandon ship and let it sink to ensure a total loss. The aftermath saw MV *Tasi* anchored in a bay with its lee weather deck still awash. As soon as she anchored, I declared "general average", an old maritime law that allows the captain to jettison some cargo to save the ship and remaining cargo.

Some hatches were opened and a barge sporting a mobile crane was moored on the low side. Nets of bagged cement were lifted out of the hold and landed on the barge, from where a helicopter lifted the nets and flew them to the shore to be repalletized and trucked to Nelson. However, this was a very slow and expensive process. After several days, permission was obtained from the NZ Marine Department to move the ship—still at a horrendous list—to Nelson.

MV *Tasi* safely anchored

Eventually the Nelson wharf labourers finished the discharge at astronomically high cost, including danger money. When finally floating upright, it was found that the stresses had warped the hull, thereby misaligning the engines and propeller shaft and damaging the unusual gearbox that joined the two main engines to the one propeller shaft. In other words, the gearbox was damaged to a point that a complete new one was needed.

The builder of the gearbox had long since closed and a new one would cost more than the ship was worth. The bureaucrats descended on the scene: Marine Department, average adjusters, underwriters of cargo and hull and the Protection and Indemnity Club representatives. After lengthy deliberations lasting over one year, MV *Tasi* was towed to

Tonga. Finally, the insurers decided to write off the ship and she was towed to the breakers.

Barge and helicopter to discharge cargo without capsizing

Another major mistake was listening to a good Norwegian friend, Fritjof Platou, who had worked at the Nordic Bank when I was a customer. He had since branched out into merchant banking. His father-in-law was a ship's captain and Fritjof thought it would be a good idea if we entered into a joint venture to buy a vessel to trade in the Pacific and employ his father-in-law as ship's master. We formed a company, Starfish Shipping, in tax-free Vanuatu. We planned to start a liner service from Tonga, Samoa and other islands to Honolulu to where many South Pacific Polynesians had migrated and now lived.

Fritjof and his father-in-law looked around for a suitable ship. We expected to load plenty of deck cargo in the form of second-hand cars and larger vehicles; so they chose a clear flush deck ship with no hatch coamings of about 2,200 tons. A number of joined pontoons, opening in concertina fashion, made up the hatches. However, sealing the pontoons to prevent water entering the holds became a problem, which was never entirely solved. Starfish Shipping bought MV *Vili* (mentioned earlier) in January 1979 for $US1,000,000, borrowing $US685,000 from Nordic Bank. Fritjof and I financed the rest equally. MV *Vili* had been built in Sweden in 1967, originally named MV *Marin*, then MV *Nogi*.

MV *Vili* (ex-MV *Nogi*) fully loaded

We could not find a delivery cargo from the Baltic towards Tonga, so we sailed to Gdansk in Poland and bought a full cargo of cement to sell in the South Pacific. It was winter and the ship was icebound in Gdansk for some time before escaping to the North Atlantic sailing towards Panama. The warmer Atlantic currents melted the ice, which had sealed the hatch pontoons. Stormy seas washed over the weather deck and water found its way into the hold of bagged cement to ruin the cargo and nearly sink the ship. Fortunately, the bilge pumps handled the slurry of cement, much of which was pumped over the side.

12. The slippery slope

Adding to our delivery problems was the world oil crisis that pushed the price of diesel up 400% from about $100 per ton to $400 per ton, during the period of the delivery voyage. On arrival in Tonga, we used jackhammers to extract the remaining solid cement from the lower hold. We had spent about $200,000 on delivery costs after a nightmare voyage budgeted to take 55 days but eventually extending to 120 days. The result was the ship had a book value of $1.2 million and a market value of $850,000. Not a good start!

The Honolulu service was a disaster, there being insufficient cargo or income to cover the cost of the long voyage, especially now that the cost of fuel had quadrupled. Despite other efforts, including five or six charter voyages, carrying bulk grain cargoes from various Australian ports to Papua New Guinea in 1981, and trading to Kiribati in 1982, we lost a further $110,000. A decision was made to sell the ship. A cargo was arranged to China, but unfortunately, when we were nearly there, an engine failure forced her to anchor off the China coast. MV *Vili* was then taken in tow by a large Chinese salvage tug that towed her at 11 knots. Although not at any risk of sinking whilst at anchor, the tug owners (that is, the Chinese authorities) claimed salvage. She was held at the port of Tongu (near Tianjin) for several months of the winter, with snow and ice on deck, and two armed guards on the gangway 24 hours per day. (This was all pre the Tiananmen Square incident.) Eventually the "salvage claim" was settled by selling the ship to the claimants at the right price, and thus the crew were allowed to fly home to Tonga in April 1987.

Bigger problems were to emerge. The Sydney shipping agent was Hetherington Kingsbury, a well-established company managed by the late Stuart Dean. They also managed some Australian coastal vessels that carried bulk sugar from the Clarence River to Sydney. Because of the over manning and huge salaries of Australian crews, these small ships became uneconomic. Stuart used to say that it would be cheaper to load the sugar into wheelbarrows and push them to Sydney rather than incur the cost of loading and delivery by an Australian manned and flagged vessel.

As road transport took over this trade, the ships became surplus and Hetherington agreed to bareboat[1] charter them to Warner Pacific Line. The flag was changed to Tonga and 16 feather-bedded Australian crew members were replaced by nine Tongans who were delighted to use all the Irish linen table cloths and well-appointed galley and

---

[1]   Bareboat—no crew.

entertainment facilities. The ships had been well maintained but were old. They were shallow drafted and not big, enabling them to ride over the bars at the entrance to NSW Northern Rivers. MV *Poolta* of 3,280 dwt was one that comes to mind.

MV *Kali*—ex MV *Poolta*

MV *Kali*—salt charter to Pago Pago, March 1985

We changed the name to MV *Kali* in 1985. It served Warner Pacific Line well for some years until, unfortunately, on one voyage on the way from the Cook Islands to Auckland in 1988, the captain decided to go fishing by trolling close to the reefs near the Kermadec Islands, north of New Zealand. He came too close and bounced the ship onto a rocky shelf and bent the tail shaft, propeller and rudder before refloating. She limped very slowly into Auckland.

The cost of repairs in New Zealand would have been uneconomical given the age of the vessel, so Hetherington sold it cheaply to a gentleman from the Arab Emirates. After temporary repairs, she departed Auckland for the Gulf, now renamed MV *Ali*, using some of our Tongan crew. The new owner went happily to the Auckland airport and flew home. However, the MV *Ali* only proceeded to the outer anchorage of Auckland and anchored as previously and secretly arranged by us with the Captain. She remained a couple of days until certain money matters were settled to our satisfaction, and duly departed and reached the Gulf. Most of the Tongan crew flew home from there. Thus ended this profitable ship for Warner Pacific Line.

Hetherington had also financed the purchase of a small tanker for Warner Pacific Line with which to deliver fuel around the islands and especially to the Cook Islands. We named it MT *Lali* and brought it all the way from Durban in South Africa to Tonga. Unlike modern tankers, it had a single skin and if the hull leaked, as it did, seawater mixed with the cargo.

This did not impress the cargo owners who lodged cargo claims. We mothballed the ship and finally towed it to Kaohsiung in Taiwan to be scrapped by the ship breakers who flourished there.

MV *Avondale*, built 1956, served well until 1984

This was an interesting tow. MV *Sami II* acted as tug and towed both MV *Tasi* and MT *Lali*, one behind the other. Hetherington had bareboat chartered both *Kali* and *Lali* to Warner Pacific Line. Because they did not make a profit, the charter money was not paid and the hire bill mounted. Hetherington became the biggest creditor but still showed confidence in the Line.

Captain Latu Lui of *Sami II*—fishing slows the voyage

12. The slippery slope

The last relatively big ship bareboat chartered from an English owner was the aforementioned MV *Sami II* (2,906 dwt tons). At 81 metres long, she had the capacity to carry up to 80 containers, but insufficient cargo gear to lift them. So, to be used as a container ship, shore cranes were needed to both load and unload the 20 foot containers. First delivered to us in Valparaiso, Chili, she was used to carry break bulk cargo on our expanding regular services. Bill Cole (whom you will read more about in the next chapter), Warner Pacific Line's shore superintendent at the New Zealand end, fitted two better derricks in 1994.

With a number of our vessels, we made inroads into the Cook Island/New Zealand trade, which we had started with the very small MV *Timo*.

MV *Timo*—employed around the Cook Islands and Niue

As we became more involved with container ships, MV *Sami II* was deployed on a contract to carry containers of lime from Tauranga, New Zealand to the gold mine at Misima in New Guinea. This kept this ship fully employed until it was due for special survey in Auckland in 1997.

Many cargo owners insisted that Warner Pacific Line modernise and enter the container shipping world, thereby contributing to the spread of large steel boxes all around the globe. To enter the container shipping world one needed not only a suitable bigger ship with good stability, but also a fleet of waterproof containers. One could buy and/or hire both.

161

MV *Timo* discharging by tug and barge on Niue 1990

***Moana II*—another Dammers sister ship**

Most of the island ports we serviced had no container cranes so the container ships had to be self-geared with derricks or cranes to lift at least 22 tons to swing full containers well out over the side of the ship without capsizing the ship. To learn more about the container business, in 1985, Warner Pacific Line undertook a short time charter of MV *Rex Star*. This was a Panama registered ship with Japanese officers and Korean crew. One of our young Tongan captains, Eduati Lemoto, sailed as supercargo to police the operation.

***Rex Star* our introduction to container shipping**

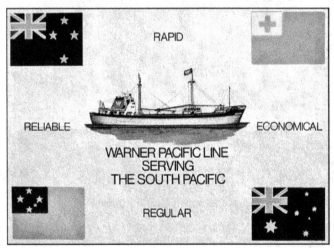

RAPID

RELIABLE

ECONOMICAL

WARNER PACIFIC LINE
SERVING
THE SOUTH PACIFIC

REGULAR

Ship-wise it all seemed to work and the trade just covered the time charter cost. Ashore was different. We soon learned that one needed to hire three sets of containers, one set onboard, one set being stuffed at the export country and one set being unstuffed at the receiving ports, plus a few that disappeared into the tropical jungles never to be seen again. Fortunately, the condition of most of the roads at the island ports prevented the overloaded trucks from disappearing too far. Keeping track of the containers was a full-time job for a studious and dedicated clerk who could distinguish between false and true reports from island agents.

MV *Rex Star* was replaced with a cheaper bareboat charter of MV *Capricornia,* the biggest ship of the Line at 4,950 dwt tons, which had two heavy lift cranes with which to load and discharge. The ship was used on both the Australian and New Zealand run to Tonga and Samoa. Stability was always a problem with this ship.

Before off-hiring MV *Capricornia* we entered into a slot charter arrangement with Sofrana Line to carry Warner Pacific Line containers on Sofrana's bigger ships. The MV *Capricornia* was off-hired and Warner Pacific Line utilized "cargo slots" on Sofrana ship *Capitaine Cook* on a monthly service to Tonga.

Small heavy lift Dutch freighter on charter at Niue wharf on a calm day

The antics and exploits of small shipping operators in the South Pacific were extremely colourful from the end of World War II through to the 1990s, by which time most had been gobbled up by world dominated liner services.

I could fill a book with their exploits but the outstanding two were Gaspard (Bill) Ravel and his mate Alain Munch, two Frenchmen who started Sofrana Unilines registered in the Wallis Islands. They first engineered and operated a monopoly shipping service between Noumea and the French outposts of Wallis and Futuna Islands.

MV *Timo* carried lighter cargo from Tonga

Originally, from Marseille, Bill Ravel had been Sergeant in Charge of the quartermaster's store in the Foreign Legion stationed in Noumea. He polished his negotiating skills where petty corruption was prevalent. It is said he cornered the supply of French officers' formal tri-cornered hats before Bastille Day celebration marches, and then sold them at outrageous prices to the officers.

Alain Munch was from Alsace, and looked like a tall German rather than a Frenchman. He had been an officer in the French navy and commander of a small warship stationed in Noumea. After leaving the military, the two men acquired their first vessel. I bought their second vessel (MV *Capitaine Cook*) when it became too small for their expanding business, and also because it was banned from returning to Mata-Utu by the local judge.

A ships' agent told me that on the following day, Munch appeared before the judge and, in the most arrogant manner, with his feet resting on the ledge of the witness box, first accused the judge of being a homosexual and then said he would not accept any verdict from this judge. He was thrown back into the cell by the only gendarme on the island. The ship was ready to sail but the captain was locked up. The motley, poorly dressed, colourful crew, originating from all outposts of the French Empire, decided to spring the captain from the jail. Armed with big marlin spikes, crow bars, axes and other implements, they marched to the jail, in a scene that was reminiscent of the French revolution.

On seeing the motley crew advancing, the one and only gendarme fled to the jungle and the crew extracted the captain. The ship sailed post haste. Before returning on the next voyage, a full platoon of gendarmes had been flown in from Noumea to greet the ship and lock Alain Munch up again, this time with plenty of guards in attendance. Here Alain waited for his partner Bill to extract him.

Sami II—Fast ride downstream during 1996 Clarence River flood

Having learned why his ship was delayed, Bill Ravel bought a quantity of alluring black negligees for the mistress of the Governor of Wallis Island and flew there without delay. After lengthy negotiations with the Governor it was agreed to release Alain on condition that neither the ship nor Alain would return again. Hence, the ship was for sale when I first met Alain Munch in Suva. He and his partner Bill had decided that Alain should be based there to attend to an expanded shipping service they had started from Sydney to Fiji and Noumea.

Alain had also married a beautiful Rotuman girl and bought a house near Suva. Sofrana Line and Warner Pacific Line shared the same port agent in Suva so I frequently met him. Jokingly over the years, I used to tell him that he was the only honest Frenchman I had ever met. This turned out to be inaccurate. Never did I trust Bill Ravel who was always trying to encroach on my trade. In our business dealings, I had understood that Warner Pacific Line would stay out of Fiji if Sofrana would stay out of Tonga and Samoa.

The relationship between the two Sofrana directors and me is akin to the story of the spider and the fly. By 1988, when I was suffering severe cash shortages, a run of ship problems, and the inability to carry heavy containers, the spider Bill Ravel said to the fly, Peter Warner, put your containers on my ships and we will divert the Sofrana vessels to call at Nuku'alofa. I had to accept and reroute MV *Capricornia* out of New Zealand to Tonga and Samoa, to the Cook Island service.

Sami II crossing the bar of the Clarence River in flood

Alain Munch and Bill Ravel had another serious argument and Alain resigned. Bill Ravel sold Sofrana Line in 1997 to Delmas, a large French shipping company which replaced some old Sofrana Line vessels with newer, bigger ships and stopped calling at Nuku'alofa from Australia. This finished the WP Line trade out of Australia.

Then in 1997 Alain Munch bought his own ships and started Neptune Shipping and carried Warner Pacific Line containers on a slot basis from New Zealand to Tonga. This enabled WP Line to cancel its charter of MV *Capricornia*, which was having serious stability problems. Later, Pacific Direct Line, whose CEO was Bill Ravel's nephew, chartered the MV *Capricornia* and renamed it MV *Polynesian Link*. She rolled over at the wharf in Suva whilst stevedores attempted to swing two loaded containers outboard simultaneously. She was finally cut into pieces to remove her from the wharf.

MV *Capricornia*

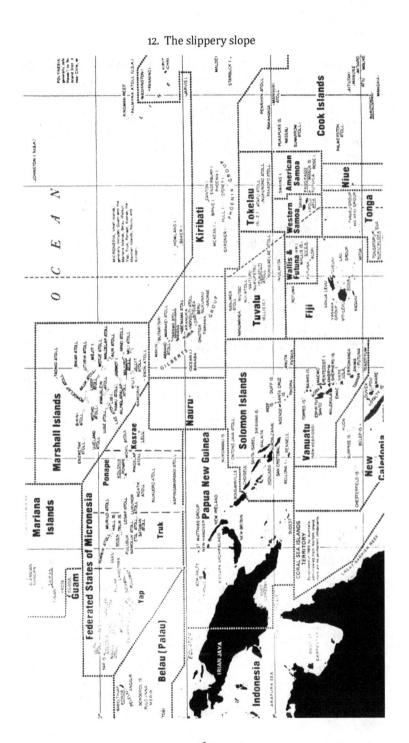

Finally, the last two "bullets" to kill the Warner Pacific Line were fired. Bill Ravel and Alain Munch renewed their friendship like a couple of old rogues. Bill persuaded Alain to cancel the slot arrangement, so they could finally kill Warner Pacific Line and carry the cargo on their own bills of lading to Tonga. The last bullet or *coup de grace* came when the MV *Sami II* was docked in Auckland in 1997. Built in East Germany, in 1972 she needed plenty of repairs to pass the special survey. The cash position was stretched.

I could not ask Hetherington for support because Warner Pacific Line had stopped trading to Australia and, already, Hetherington bills were overdue. Warner Pacific Line was a month in arrears with the bareboat charter payments on *Sami II*. I asked the English owner to visit me at the Auckland dock and explained the situation. To avoid having the ship arrested by the shipyard, he agreed to cancel the charter and take over the docking and survey costs. He kept and paid the Warner Pacific Line crew and we parted company amicably.

So by 1997 I was left with no ships and the cargo flow generated over 25 exciting years had been hi-jacked and gone to others. *C'est la vie!*

13
Personalities of
Warner Pacific Line

13
Personalities of Warner Pacific Line

Over the many years in fishing and shipping one enjoyed the company and was assisted by many helpers, agents, crews, captains, engineers and marine supervisors. There were too many to mention all. I can only vaguely remember some, like Eduati Lemoto, Ditty Wendt, Uiki Ofa, Jock Maestri, Mikio Filitonga and Harold Newman. However, some remain strongly imbedded in my memory and are worth a mention.

First to mind was Captain Mosesi Haukinima, known as Hau for short, from Felemea on the Ha'apai island of 'Uiha. He had started his life in sailing type cutters and whalers. He was first master of *Just David*. Instinctively he always steered around the lee side of any object. He taught me many Polynesian navigational tips including how to smell an approaching reef in the night. He taught me the Tongan names for stars and constellations and I taught him how to use a chart and ultimately the use of sextant and stopwatch for European style celestial navigation. This was before the days of GPS and very few little ships had radar.

Captain Hau never overloaded his vessels with passengers and never hit a reef. He possessed a great sense of humour and enjoyed teasing crew and passengers. Early one morning he came out of the wheelhouse, looked at the sky and asked the deck passengers dozing on the wing of the bridge if they had seen any birds. "Why?" said the passengers, to which Hau responded, "Because we are lost, so if you see any come and tell me." After about 15 minutes, a worried passenger burst into the wheel house and yelled "Look over there to the right there are a few birds flying." With tongue in cheek, Hau bellowed to the helmsman, "Hard a starboard and follow the birds!" Of course, he was not lost but the passenger thought he had helped to save the ship.

On other occasions, Hau would stroll around the deck with a furled Tongan flag under one arm and a bible under the other looking for seasick deck passengers too ill to move in their misery. He would drape the flag over the still body and take out his bible to read the burial service in Tongan. "Ashes to ashes, dust to dust" he would intone in a deep and religious voice. It was surprising how many startled, sick passengers pretended to instantly recover. He finally retired and went to live with some of his family in Brisbane.

Captain Hau with "Seagull", alias Peter Junior

Next is Bill Cole who had sailed with me before I came to Tonga and then joined me on the MV *Ata* on her maiden voyage to Tonga. He was an electrician and served his apprenticeship at the Devonport Naval Dock in Auckland. He enjoyed the simple pleasures of life including yacht sailing but was always ready for a challenge when required. His domineering half-Russian, half-Welsh mother and a stubborn English father produced a tenacious son who was my right-hand man, dealing with recalcitrant crewmembers and technical problems. He was devoted to his children whom I saw grow up. He and his capable wife Linda came to live in Tonga and raised two children. He helped supervise the maintenance of the growing Warner Pacific Line fleet.

The Tongans love teasing and tried to test Bill's patience on many occasions. The crew would see him walking down the wharf towards a Warner Pacific Line ship and run down to the engine room, remove a few tools from the neatly stowed shadow board and leave them randomly scattered around the deck. Of course, they should have been at work, but produced guitars and sat playing and singing on the hatch cover as Bill approached. Spotting a tool laying on deck, Bill would point and ask "What's that doing there?" and nobody would know the answer, as the teasing musicians tried to fuel his fury. They often succeeded and, not until he had his own children, did he understand this childish technique. After ten exciting years based in Tonga, he moved back to Auckland to resume his job as a supervisor. Amongst other challenges he skilfully handled the salvage of MV *Tasi* after its near capsize described earlier.

Bill joined me from the very start of the Warner Pacific Line and even went to Japan to participate in the delivery voyage of MV *Frysna* in 1972. When Warner Pacific Line finished he became a shore superintendent with Sofrana Unilines and later Neptune Shipping.

Ashore in Tonga, I had some great helpers. Kevin Davids came from Burns Philp where he had started work in 1956 as a young man in their Bridge St, Sydney Office in the Islands Department. In 1968, he became a purser on MV *Bulolo*, which was, at the time, the flagship of the BP Shipping Line under the late Captain Brett Hilder. In 1972, he was seconded to BP Fiji as an accountant. He later served in Pago Pago and Niue Island. He finally decided to end his BP Shipping Line days and do his own thing, but after a stint ashore in Queensland, he joined Warner Pacific Line in Tonga as an accountant and office manager.

Kevin worked with me from 1981 to 1994 both in Tonga and later in Sydney where he set up the Australian Institute of Studies, an English Language school for overseas students. There were not many in this world like him. Where can one find someone who is loyal, patient, and tolerant, loved his wife and knew how to keep a secret? For me he was a blessing. Unfortunately, he was a heavy smoker and died of cancer after a long illness in 1999.

I developed a method of training hopefuls into becoming ships officers, engineers, electricians and shore managers by starting a cadet training scheme. There is a famous Wesleyan boarding school named Toloa College. Supeli Taliai was the experienced principal whom I befriended. I would ask him to find possible candidates for cadet training from his list of students undertaking their last year at high school.

I would explain to Supeli that I was looking for brave, healthy young men who could climb coconut palms, swim and catch fish, rather than the more studious types who thought they knew everything. Those that had just failed their final examinations were more trainable for a hard life rather than those who were top of the class.

Amongst these candidates was Maake Fakaosifolau who had studied bookkeeping at school. Amongst his early duties, was auditing the fish and barge stores in Ha'apai anchorages. Here at the age of 19 he fell in love with the daughter of one of the Catholic fishermen on 'Uiha island and eloped with her in a dinghy and outboard headed towards the main town in Ha'apai on Lifuka island. The angry father of the bride was in hot pursuit in another boat trying to stop his Catholic daughter marrying the Methodist boy. However, he was too late. Maake found a preacher to marry them hastily before her father caught up. I believe they are still married 45 years later. Maake and I grew close over the years. He took over the ships agency office when I departed from Tonga, and divided his time between shipping and growing large amounts of root crops.

Toimoana Takataka was another former student of Toloa College, who came to work as a clerk. He came from a Vava'u family of planters and was married young to Lita from Ma'ufanga. After some training, I sent him to Apia in Samoa to act as owner's representative at the ships agency owned by Thor Netzler and his wife. Toi, as he was known, soon learned to use the Samoan language fluently. He knew all the tricks tried by our Samoan shippers, customs officers, stevedores and petty bureaucrats.

The practice in Apia was to discharge the palletized cargo onto a wharf and carry it down to the customs shed where consignees came with their paper work and trucks to haul it away. The shed was locked at night by the customs officers. Cargo mysteriously disappeared at all points. First, the young stevedores would pilfer as much as possible inside the holds even when our crew were on guard and, then, cargo that was locked in the shed at night was not there in the morning. Toi counted the stock most likely to be pillaged, like cigarettes and canned corn beef before the shed was closed and again the next morning. He concluded that the Customs officials were involved in the cargo disappearance and asked me to confront the Collector of Customs on the subject. This I did by asking, "Can we post a watchman in the locked shed overnight?" "No," replied the Collector "because there may be a fire and the watchman could not escape". "OK can we lock some fierce dogs in the shed overnight?" "No, because the dogs would tear up too many cartons and make a mess," said the Collector. "Well," said I, "the Romans used geese to guard their property and they make a big honking noise if disturbed, so can we lock some caged geese inside?" "No", replied the Collector, "because there are no geese in Samoa and quarantine would not permit their import."

He obviously knew that we knew what was happening and the disappearance of cargo slowed down for a few more months. However, eventually there was a mysterious fire, and the whole shed and its contents with all the relevant records were destroyed. Thereafter consignees could take their cargo from the wharf apron direct from the ships slings. That was before another shed was built by foreign aid.

Kava grew well in Samoa, but the growers received poor prices compared to Tonga where the root was very much in demand. As a private sideline business, Toi started buying dried kava roots from the Samoans to ship in sacks to his young wife in Tonga. Lita and her family would bundle the roots into small parcels and sell them day and night to the Kava drinking club members. This grew into a big business. Finally, Toi said to me that he wanted to resign and move to Vava'u to grow kava on his father's land. He did this and became a wealthy Tongan and the biggest Tongan kava grower. He was a quiet sensible operator and always cheerful to all comers who were not trying to cheat him.

Granville Kirton gets a mention in the chapter on how I became a Bahá'í. I enjoyed the friendship of many other people in and about Tonga but this chapter only refers to a very few amongst those who worked at Warner Pacific Line.

14
Tavi

14
Tavi

At the age of 30, Preben Vigo Heinrich Kaufmann, later to become known as only as Tavi, arrived in Tonga in his 28-foot yacht from San Francisco sometime in 1953. This young Danish hydraulics engineer and would-be hermit had sailed singlehanded across the Pacific and had fallen in love with Tonga. He gave his yacht to Queen Sālote in return for the privilege of living on any of a selected number of uninhabited Tongan islands.

This brilliant young engineer and mathematician was pessimistic about the progress of the world. He thought nothing good would come of modern civilization. He rejected everything from money to modern gadgets and was satisfied with his life as a hermit.

Tavi would travel hither and yon between the islands in government boats and later free-of-charge on Warner Pacific Line. He homed in and lived very simply, first on the uninhabited island of Hunga Tonga and later on the high island of Tafahi near Niuatoputapu. On waking in his lean-to or cave, he would drink the dew from leaves and devour a whole ripe papaya (paw-paw). Over the years, the regular dose of the papaya's yellow flesh, which is full of carotene, eventually turned the palms of his hands and the whites of his eyes yellow.

During the mornings, Tavi would fish or tend his small vegetable garden. Sometime during the day, he would make a meal of some roots, fish and leaves. He was very healthy except for a heart problem. When I first met him, this tall skinny pale Dane had grown a wispy beard in which cockroaches tried to nest whilst he was asleep. His solution to this irritation was to place a tilted jar of fermented coconut cream near his head. The cockroaches would be more attracted to the coconut and fall and drown in the coconut milk.

I recall carrying some high school students to his island for tutoring in higher mathematics, such as calculus and trigonometry, which he taught them by sketching formulas with a pointed stick in the wet sand at low tide. They would stay with him until we made another visit. I asked him if there was anything he wanted from the outside world. He said he missed toothpaste as the ashes from his fire were too gritty, and he longed for music. On the next voyage, I brought him a portable radio, a good supply of batteries and some toothpaste.

Other than some stored gold coins that he had been given by his mother, he had no use for money. On one occasion, when asked to act as temporary director of the Public Works Department, he refused to accept any payment. Anytime the government needed him to undertake engineering projects they sent a boat to find him. He designed and built a Danish-style church in one village that has withstood many earthquakes.

Perhaps because we were both nautically experienced, or because we were both disillusioned by the way the mid-20th century was progressing, we struck up a friendship even though he was completely eccentric and stubborn. His close rapport with the royal family entitled him the right to be the only European to enter the Palace anytime without the guards throwing him out. When his mother visited, Queen Sālote hosted her. Tavi's father was Danish and his Mother a high German. Born in 1901, her name, Ingeborg von Kauffmann, reflected her stern domineering and very conservative outlook. At a garden party at the Palace, I recall her watching the well-dressed brass band playing in the rotunda and the smartly uniformed Tongan Military Officers in their polished Sam Brown belts strolling about with swagger sticks. She remarked loudly, with a German accent, "This reminds me of the good old days of the German Empire, when there was some law and order in the country." Is it any wonder Tavi wanted to be a hermit?

Tavi once accompanied me on a voyage to Australia where I had a hydraulic engineering problem to solve and needed his advice. I wanted to collect rain from a wet headland and direct it by pipe to a dam to be built on the dry family cattle breeding station located on a peninsula near Bowen, Queensland. (Read more about Cape Upstart in the third part of my autobiography.)

After an inspection, Tavi made all the calculations and, when it rained on the headland, the captured water flowed successfully in the right size pipe he had designed. However, the east coast of Australia then experienced three years of drought and it took four years to fill the large dam that we built at the dry end of the pipeline. My teenage son, Peter, helped dig the long pipeline.

Whilst in Sydney, my medical student daughter brought her fascinated student friends to listen to Tavi's murmuring heart.

Apparently, one valve was not closing properly but he refused to undergo surgery to fix it even though doctors recommended open heart surgery. In the city of Sydney, he could be seen dressed as a Tongan in his lap lap (*vala*), sandals, open neck shirt, and sporting a long white wispy beard.

As he grew older and his weak heart handicapped his manual activities, Tavi eventually returned to live on the main island in Tonga amongst people. He occupied a converted cement water tank supplied by me. His tank home was located on the waterfront near Touliki where he watched the world go by and read many books. He came to realize that he could not become totally free from an advancing globalized civilization.

Finally, in 1992, Tavi sailed to Auckland on MV *Timo* where he remained until the Danish Consul arranged free repatriation to Denmark, where he lived with his sister on a pension until his death about the turn of the century. He was a talented man whose skills were not fully used. For those interested to learn more about Tavi, a Danish journalist, Leif Moller, wrote an account of his life in 2006 entitled *Tavi fra Tonga*, but it is in Danish.

Tavi as a young man

15
Proposed schooner for the two Niuas and Tokelau Islands

15
Sailing ship proposal for the
two Niuas and Tokelau Islands

When fuel prices quadrupled in the 1970s, there was much talk about the return to sail in commercial shipping. Wind is free; why then pay for fuel! The concept did not work for large ships that had to keep tight schedules or where the economy of scale and latest fuel-saving devices showed that fuel was not a large cost factor per ton of cargo in the movement of big cargo shipments of, say, 200,000 tons of coal in one ship. However, in smaller ships servicing remote islands, it was a different story. Often, Warner Pacific Line ships and others wasted fuel and time manoeuvring backwards and forwards offshore of many islands whilst waiting for favourable weather, so that we could land cargo and passengers with surfboats or negotiate tricky reef passages. The cost of fuel and other consumable items slowly increased whilst waiting offshore. Large vessels on scheduled liner services cannot afford to engage in such time and fuel wasting exercises, so smaller vessels are usually assigned this job.

In the last two centuries, private trading schooners and missionary boats serviced these islands, but such vessels became scarcer in the late 20th century. Warner Pacific Line endeavoured to service Niuafo'ou and Niuatoputapu *en route* from New Zealand via Tonga to Samoa and return. However, although our ships passed close to these two islands on the northbound and southbound passages, often weather prevented landing passengers and cargo. The passengers and perishable cargo would be carried on to the next safe port so they could not always rely on such a service.

During the 1970s, the World Council of Churches had money to advance for worthwhile projects. Tongan churches were a recipient member. Father Kali (his Tongan name) was an energetic and enthusiastic French priest who had spent many years on Niuafo'ou, starting as a young priest, eventually becoming a respected elder. He spoke the language, a mixture of Samoan, Uvean and Tongan. Due to his efforts, the population was predominantly Catholic.

Niuafo'ou, an unusual northern-most island in the Tongan group, was a round volcanic cone with a warm crater lake 25 metres above sea level with a depth of 90 metres. The island was completely surrounded by cliffs and landing by surfboat was difficult. There were no sheltering reefs and marine people refer to it as "steep to" and almost impossible to anchor in the close deep water. For years, it was also known as "Tin Can Island" because of a brave inhabitant who used to swim out to passing liners with the mail in a tin can. Volcanic eruptions occurred: a big one in 1886 started a huge fire and another explosive one in 1946 caused the evacuation of the total population who were relocated to the Eua Island. Suffering from the cold in this most southerly Tongan island, some survivors returned to rebuild Niuafo'ou in 1958. I believe the population in 2006 was 650.

With the help of the Bishop, the French Father Kali pursued the World Council of Churches in Geneva for money with which to build a hospital on this remote island. A hospital was essential even though the good Catholic nuns ran a free clinic for the sick, especially those who did not find the cures they wanted from the local witch doctors. However, the council rejected the application because, apart from the initial financial outlay, the maintenance and staffing expenses would be an ongoing cost that the council could not promise to cover forever.

Undaunted, the next application by Father Kali was for a school but it met with the same answer. Who would guarantee the continuing costs? Finally, the idea of a shipping service came up. Warner Pacific Line had been servicing this island when weather permitted whilst sailing between Tonga and Samoa, but not in a reliable way. Passengers and perishable cargo did not appreciate being carried over to other ports.

Father Kali and I had a friendly working relationship, right from my first visit to Niuafo'ou on the 45-foot *Just David*, which had been chartered by the Mormons to land some starry-eyed missionaries who did not last too long in this Catholic stronghold. Father Kali was enthusiastic about my idea of a sailing ship to service Niuafo'ou and Niuatoputapu at no ongoing cost to the Council of Churches, other than the initial cost of building a vessel to my design.

I made the calculations based on the actual revenue earned by the Warner Pacific Line in 1978 from servicing these islands less the estimated cost of operating the sailing ship based on the known running costs of a similar sized ship (MV *Ata*). It all seemed viable if the Churches built and owned the ship to be a bareboat chartered to Warner Pacific Line for, say, 10 years at, say, $1 per day. My naval architect (my nephew Andrew Warner) came up with a plan for a 3-mast staysail schooner of 410 tons displacement with a water line length of 111 feet. This vessel could also act as a cadet training ship for future crews; so I was excited.

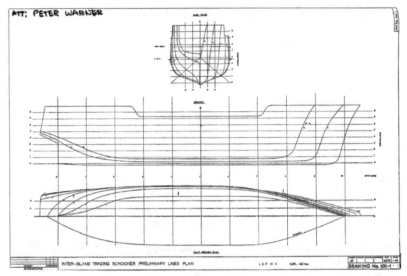

Inter-island trading schooner preliminary line plans: Drawing no. 100-1

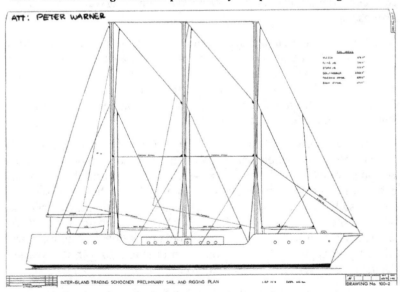

Inter-island trading schooner preliminary sail and rigging plan: Drawing no. 100-2

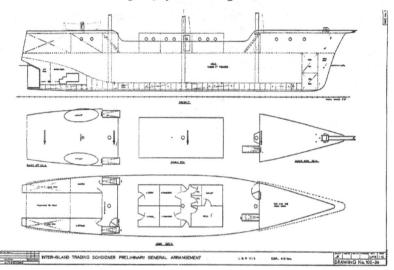

**Inter-island trading schooner preliminary general arrangement:
Drawing no. 100-3a**

Finally, in June 1979, I submitted the proposal to the World Council of Churches via Bishop Finau. However slow committees generally are in their deliberations, church committees can be even slower. Then, two coincidental events that occurred soon afterwards halted the proposal forever.

Firstly, Father Kali had been losing his sight for some time. Before my next visit to Niuafo'ou, the Bishop handed me a confidential letter to be delivered by hand to the Father—which I did willingly, not knowing the contents. Behold, it was an order to leave his lifetime's work and retire to France immediately for medical attention. He was to return to Nuku'alofa immediately on our vessel.

The news spread quickly on the island. When it was time to leave in the surfboat, the whole island community gathered on the shore, weeping to see their beloved Father embarking with all his worldly possessions. After nearly a full lifetime on the island, he possessed only a small suitcase and an umbrella. It was an extremely moving sight as his flock thought it would be the last time they would see him. Was it salt spray or tears in his eyes as he waved to the hymn-singing crowd while we crested the first line of ocean breakers to join the Warner Pacific Line vessel standing by offshore?

As it turned out, he went to France where cataracts were removed from his eyes. After a long absence, he came back to Tonga but remained on the main island of Tongatapu, where amongst other duties, he supervised the construction of a large Catholic basilica and became the French Consul. Before he was medically retired to France, he had become a major ramrod for the sailing ship project and his promotion of the cause was lost when he departed.

The other event that stopped the sailing ship venture was that the institutions that backed the World Council of Churches financially lost faith in the conduct of the Council. There was a widely reported scandal concerning their support of a Marxist guerrilla group in Africa. Its reputation sank and funds ran out. Our sailing ship plan sank together with the finances of the World Council of Churches. Yet, such a proposal would still be viable and beneficial today.

Following my last visit to Niuafo'ou in 1996 with Crown Prince Tupouto'a, I wrote a report for the Tongan Government on boosting the economic development of the two Niuas. A copy of this report is included in Appendix 3 as an addendum to this book.

16
How I became a Bahá'í

16
How I became a Bahá'í

During my seafaring days, and before I was married at the age of 25, I had come in contact with many cultures and religions in faraway ports. Buddhism, Hinduism, Confucianism, Islám, Judaism and others all intrigued me. I read whatever English translations of their holy writings were available, visited temples, and listened to priests who could speak English.

At first, I was sceptical, having been schooled in a Christian Church of England run establishment where the school chaplain insisted that only the Church of England had a monopoly on the key to heaven. Even Catholics were not to be regarded as strictly Christian. Obviously, the rest of the world did not agree. It became a hobby and challenge for me to read the holy writings of as many religions as possible, which broadened my spiritual outlook. It appeared that although some religions had many so-called gods (e.g. Hinduism), they all believed in only one Creator.

By the time I was married, I had already experienced two near-death events, had prayed and survived. There is nothing like this to concentrate the mind on whether there is a Creator or not. It is impossible to prove the existence of God logically, but likewise it is impossible to prove that there is no God. I decided at this early stage of my life on this planet to study further and hedge my bets by accepting that there was a Saviour. It would not matter if I was wrong, but if I was right, I might progress further on my eternal journey after death.

My comparative readings of all these holy writings revealed that all the Founders of those religions taught much the same lessons: They promoted love, trust, charity, justice and many other godly though latent human values. I started to believe that any religion is better than no religion, in that they all teach important values for the betterment and improvement of mankind.

I was not sure if I was a physical being having a spiritual experience or a spiritual being having a physical experience. However, having married a good Christian lady who wanted our children raised as Christians, I thought I had better shut up about my inner broad beliefs and tow the Christian line, which I did until I met a Bahá'í in Tonga.

Grenville Kirton was an Englishman and a bachelor who came to work with me as our office manager and accountant in the Nuku'alofa office of the Warner Pacific Line. This well-spoken gentleman had come to live in Tonga as what is known in the Bahá'í faith as "a pioneer". A pioneer is like an unpaid missionary who has to support himself whilst working for the faith. He had experienced a strict English upbringing where the children are sent at an early age to draughty cold stone boarding schools in Scotland whilst lapdog pets are cuddled at home before warm fireplaces. He may have been an English blue blood but he projected a warm relationship to all comers.

On discovering that Grenville was a Bahá'í, I asked him one day in a flippant manner, "How many wives can a Bahá'í have?"; to which he gave me a short answer and continued working. A few days later, I asked him another question about his beliefs and again he gave me a short answer. This continued for a few weeks and his short answers made me more curious. Finally, I said, "Grenville, when are you going to tell me more about the Bahá'í Faith?"

"I am not going to give a drink to someone who is not thirsty," he replied to what he considered was another of my flippant questions.

This negative sales pitch, generated my curiosity even more, and I said, "But I am thirsty! Do you have an equivalent of, say, the Bible that I can read?"

"No, but we have many holy Writings written by the Founder Himself, and I will get you some."

He came to work with a copy of *The Kitáb-i-Íqán* or *The Book of Certitude* written by the Co-Founder of the Faith, Bahá'u'lláh, in about the mid-nineteenth century and translated into English in 1931. Fortunately, I had read the Qur'án, and had a reasonable understanding of Islám, because the book given to me referred to many Muslim quotations and practices.

Although the two Founders had been raised in Islamic countries, the Bahá'í Faith is no more Islamic than Christianity is Jewish. I devoured *The Book of Certitude* and thought to myself that this Faith cannot be a religion because it makes too much common sense.

Grenville helped explain some of the difficult parts and informed me that in the Bahá'í Faith there was no priesthood, only unsalaried elected administrators; there were no churches except for seven temples[1] scattered around the world; and assured me about latent human attributes, equality of men and women, and that religion must be in accord with science and reason.

I was hooked, but not ready to declare myself as a Bahá'í because it would create tension within my family. I became what could be called an "undercover Bahá'í". Not until all my children were married did I declare as a believer in 1990 and registered on the waiting list to make my first pilgrimage to the World Centre in Israel. There was a six-year wait but well worth it, being a beautiful experience in spiritual deepening when finally made.

There is another marvellously deep book written by Bahá'u'lláh in Bagdad after he had been exiled from Persia. It is an answer to learned questions posed to him by a judge who had a leaning towards the poetry and beliefs of Persian Sufi followers. *The Seven Valleys and the Four Valleys* guides the reader on a difficult journey through seven stages to reach the Ocean of the Life-Bestower. Soon after I declared, I shared a meal with one of the elected members of the international Bahá'í body called the Universal House of Justice who asked me what it was like to be a new believer. I replied, "I feel spiritually drunk."

"You must have jumped over the Seven Valleys in one leap," he said.

So I left Tonga spiritually enriched if money poor. Nevertheless, it can be said: "the measure of a man's riches is the fewness of his wants".[2] Having had a life of rich experiences, I think I fit into this slot.

---

[1] To date, ten Bahá'í Houses of Worship have been built around the world, including the earliest one erected in Ashgabat ('Ishqábád), Turkmenistan, which was expropriated by the government of the day and, then, destroyed by an earthquake. Nine temples currently stand, eight of which are continental temples and one is a local temple.

[2] Jack Mulholland, quoted by David Attenborough in *Life on Air: Memoirs of a Broadcaster*, p. 181, Princeton University Press, 2002.

17
Education and the launch
of Ocean of Light in Tonga

17
Education and the launch of Ocean of Light in Tonga

Education looms as one of the most important tools to the advancement of civilization. The Founder of the Bahá'í Faith emphasized and encouraged all families to educate their children to the best of the parents' ability. When money for education is short, it should be spent on educating the girls first. Why? Because they become the future mothers; and mothers are the first teachers of their children. An educated mother can capably nurture her children to develop their positive attributes. In many societies, and especially in Tonga, grandparents, uncles and aunts, are also natural educators. Amongst other things, they teach handicraft skills and culture to the girls; and fishing and farming to the boys. However, as technology advances, it is the children who teach their elders advanced technology and advanced religious beliefs.

It was with this in mind, that I came to the conclusion that a regular school teaching the government-dictated curriculum could be infused with some progressive religious teachings. This thought was the basis for promoting the school in Tonga called the "Ocean of Light" primary and then secondary school. In Tonga, all sorts of Christian sects were—and still are—vigorously promoted. In my early days in the Kingdom, I noticed that the Seventh Day Adventist Church was expanding fast, not by building more churches but by building more schools. The schools taught their faith to the kids and the kids went home and taught the faith to the parents. This seemed to work well as this sect expanded with many new Seventh Day Adventist churches appearing. This further reinforced my desire to promote a Bahá'í school which could indirectly help expand the Faith.

A Bahá'í school must also be a school of excellence in all fields. A common saying amongst Bahá'ís when planning a project is "if you cannot do it well, do not do it at all". This is a high goal to set but it follows that a high standard school attracts parents who want the best for their children. Leading up to the opening of this school in 1996, I had gained some experience in training Tongan cadet officers and engineers for the small fleet of old ships known as the Warner Pacific Line. I knew it was important to combine practical and theoretical education; and, more importantly, to inspire young people to absorb knowledge like dry sponges sucking up water.

Proficiency in the English language was a challenge. New Zealand marine examiners failed many of our cadets in their oceangoing mates and master's certificates because the trainees could not express themselves clearly enough in English. They had the practical experience to solve the examination questions, but not in English. English is the base language for international marine communication and is the language of modern technology. With the aid of an Australian aid educator, Barry, who was working with the Tongan Education Department, we set up an "English as a Second Language" (ESL) school in Nuku'alofa, mostly for our own crews but all comers were welcome. This was not an official school—just an informal gathering.

At the same time, Barry was telling me about the potentially rewarding opportunities of opening an ESL school in Sydney to cater for foreign students arriving in Australia for further education. Many student visas were being issued to young people from mainland China. To obtain a student visa for tertiary courses, the applicants had to enrol first in an accredited ESL school in Australia unless they were already proficient in the language. With Barry's help, we negotiated the corridors of Canberra bureaucracy and obtained a license to establish an ESL school, subject to paying for Australian teachers and a qualified principal.

All went to plan and paying students arrived. There was a shortage of qualified Australian ESL teachers. It has to be explained that Australian teachers are very expensive to employ. They teach only a few hours per day for 40 weeks per year and enjoy 12 weeks of paid leave during school holidays. Teaching is a noble profession but, in Australia, respect for the profession is being lost as unions dictate conditions adverse to the student's benefit.

At the time, many of these young qualified teachers were more importantly enjoying their life in Bali and only returning when necessary to teach short periods in Australia. Therefore, I went on a successful recruiting visit to Bali on my way to Surabaya for shipping business. Whilst in Surabaya, I met up with a young Bahá'í mathematics teacher who said there were also opportunities to establish ESL schools in Indonesia. I put this in the back of my mind because I knew from previous experience about all the problems and handicaps of doing anything in Indonesia.

All was going well at the ESL school in Sydney until the Tiananmen Square disaster incident in China. The Australian Government stopped issuing visas to mainland Chinese students. The source of 90% of the students dried up overnight and the school was left with expensive teachers and staff and no students. Therefore, the school had to close. The operation was left with computers, teaching materials, desks etc., so the subject of reopening with cheaper staff in Surabaya arose. Kevin Davids, an old Burns Philp man who had been with me for years as an accountant, was the director and "bean counter" behind the Sydney school. My daughter Carolyn acted as bursar. Unfortunately, neither wanted to live in Indonesia. So I appointed the honest Bahá'í mathematics teacher as principal and director of the Surabaya ESL School and shipped over the educational material.

Indonesia heads the list of the countries of "gifts" in Asia. It took many gifts to generals and bureaucrats before we had permission to open. There were plenty of enthusiastic students, mostly with Chinese backgrounds. Our dear mathematics teacher could not control the money and, when our lease on the general's school building expired, I decided to stop the money drain and close the school. By this time, I had gained some knowledge in operating schools.

Returning to the Tongan situation, in 1994 I took council with the Bahá'í National Assembly of Tonga, the Governing Council of nine who looked after the affairs of the Bahá'í community. They were enthusiastic about starting a primary school for all comers including the children of Bahá'í parents. Of course, we needed to write a lengthy application to the Ministry of Education. My job was to lobby the Ministry to move on our application

During the period before and after the launching, the Minister for Education was Dr S. L. Kaviliku, known to all as Langi. Although a minister of the Crown, he was hardly ever in Tonga. He spent most of his life enjoying postgraduate scholarships offered to the Kingdom by overseas universities. Although a very nice chap, with two very beautiful wives, one after the other, Joan and Fuiva, he delegated all his work to the Director of Education, Loupe Paul Bloomfield, known as Paula. Paula was a strict Christian and an extremely conservative bureaucrat who avoided making decisions wherever possible. He gave priority to government schools over private schools and did not favour non-Christian schools at all, even though I explained that Bahá'ís followed the teachings of Jesus amongst other Manifestations of God.

The National Assembly of Bahá'ís appointed a five-member Board of Education, which negotiated a lease over the empty offices of the Copra Board at Haveluloto. The building was big enough for our primary school but had no playing field. Splendid school buildings do not always reflect a good school. It is the teachers and staff that make the school, whether under the shade of a tree or in an air-conditioned glasshouse. In 1995, we recruited the staff including the first principal in anticipation of opening for the New Year term on 22 January 1996, at the same time as all the other schools.

I met our first principal, Barbara Hart, at a Bahá'í conference or a Bahá'í summer school sometime in early 1995. She was planning to retire as senior teacher from the services of the NSW Education Department. This highly capable lady volunteered to come to Tonga and take up the poorly paid position as principal for a minimum of two years. She managed very successfully whilst projecting a warm welcoming atmosphere to all corners. Besides her academic ability, she nurtured the young students in the best Bahá'í tradition.

Barbara Hart, first Principal top right; author, bottom right, with some early helpers

All preparations were made to open the school, but no decision was forthcoming from the Ministry of Education. The Director would not or could not make a decision. My lobbying intensified during the second half of 1995 with weekly visits or daily phone calls in January 1996 as opening day approached. The 22 January came and went and many of our recruited students enrolled at other schools, thinking we would never obtain permission to open. The pressure on me to perform for the National Spiritual Assembly of Tonga caused me to have an attack of an old recurring illness that put me to bed with a fever for five critical days from 20 January. Finally, in early March, when all other schools were fully enrolled, we were granted conditional permission to open and the first day of teaching started on Tuesday 5 March with only nine students who had remained loyal and hopeful and did not enrol in other schools. Because of the small number of paying students, I thought we were heading for a financial disaster, but slowly the enrolments increased and by term two we could see light at the end of the tunnel financially. By the second year we were full and in the third year there was a waiting list of students wanting to enrol.

PRIMARY SCHOOL

To run a school of excellence, one must pay for the best in everything, notably teachers. Our excellent teachers were backed up by young graduate volunteer tutors from Bahá'í communities worldwide. These volunteers on a year of service to the Faith helped any individual students who fell behind in their work. The combined result of good teaching, tutoring and leadership was good academic achievements overall. The cost of providing the best service was reflected in our high term fees, and the Ocean of Light Primary School became the most expensive primary school in the Kingdom. Whilst open to all comers, the majority of the student mix came from the foreign expatriate families residing in Tonga.

Originally the school was planned to help in the education of the children of local Bahá'í families. We "shot ourselves in the foot" because the high fees were not affordable to the Tongan Bahá'ís with large families. To help them we established a scholarship fund and I, amongst others, approached the Bahá'í communities in Australia to donate to this fund, so that some of the local Bahá'í kids could attend. The scholarship committee never granted a 100% funded scholarship but always asked the Bahá'í parents to pay something towards the fees even if only 10% or 20%. Something for nothing is never fully appreciated. Contributing something lifts the self-esteem of the parents or guardians.

The second obstacle was which language was to be used in teaching which subjects. Originally, we promoted a bilingual school, with some subjects like singing, Tongan history etc., being taught in Tongan and technical subjects like maths and science in English. In this way, the foreign students would learn Tongan and the Tongan students would become more proficient in English. However, because of our mix of students, teachers, volunteers and foreign students, English quickly became the common language and our early dream was discarded.

This led us to overcome the next obstacle. The youngest Tongan kids, who spoke Tongan at home, had trouble mastering English in the lower primary classes, and it became a handicap in their early learning years. To solve this, the Ocean of Light Primary School opened a preschool or kindergarten for the future year one students so they could mix in an English-speaking environment before they started school.

Of course, the Ocean of Light Primary School was keen on the latest technology and needed internet connection and computers for the children. The cost of the internet access was prohibitive at that time. Knowing that HRH the Crown Prince had orchestrated free access for his army school, I had a long audience with him on 4 March 1996.

By way of background, around that time, an international conference had agreed to allocate 360 satellite parking spaces circling the globe above the equator to countries that applied. Most parking spaces or slots were instantly taken up by big countries, but there were two left over and Tonga bid and acquired them. HRH and especially his sister Princess Pilolevu took interest in these parking spaces (slots) which later were rented out to communication companies at good prices.

HRH said he had been approached by Intel Corporation representatives who were keen to put all of Asia on the internet as soon as possible, thereby boosting their sales of chips. To do this they needed satellites. The offer was that in consideration of a Tongan slot, Tonga would get a free fast connection to the world by the year 2001, and, in particular, to universities and educational facilities.

Meanwhile, all Tongan high schools were to get free laptops and all schools free access to the internet. Unfortunately, like many plans of Tongan royalty, this did not eventuate, but it illustrates his keen interest in promoting education; and, indeed, he did the Ocean of Light

Primary School the honour of officially attending some of the school functions.

Pressure from parents of pupils finishing primary school and not wishing to find another school encouraged the Board to open a High School division with technical facilities for both local and on-line courses. Two years after the opening, I returned to Australia but followed its progress from afar by sending second-hand desks and many resources for a period of time.

The Board of Education continued to manage the school with great dedication. The school operated in the Haveluloto premises until 2003, by which time the Board acquired a six-acre piece of land and constructed two beautiful buildings, one for each of the Primary and High School divisions. The school roll progressively expanded and, to this day, the school is operating with distinction. It remains the pride and joy of the Bahá'í Community of Tonga, offering a high standard of moral and academic education to more than 350 students (in 2015) from diverse backgrounds. It is an institution where students develop a desire to learn and acquire the capacity to serve their community.

Story from the *Tonga Chronicle*, 7 March 1996, p. 2:

Bahá'ís open Ocean of Light International Primary School

By Pilimisola Tamo'au

A primary school administered by the Bahá'í Community of Tonga began its first session on Tuesday with nine class 1–3 Students.

Principal Barbara Hart, who brings 35 years of teaching experience at all levels to the post, described herself as "delighted" with the first day and found the children "so well mannered. It is a joy to work with them."

Mrs Hart of Australia and two teachers are concentrating on literacy and numeracy, following the same curriculum as that of Tonga Side School. Part-time teachers assist in music, art and sports.

Five-year-old Nani Pulini attending school for the first time in his life, said that he liked it and found it fun to play with other children. Benjamin Wise, 8, said that his first day was good, and he especially liked being "the biggest boy in the school".

Class 4–6 will be introduced next year with computer literacy as part of the curriculum, said Mr Peter Warner, a trust member. "Ocean of Light is an international school that keep its doors open for all races, rich and poor, without prejudice. Everybody in welcome," Mr Warner said.

The Ocean of Light International Primary School, occupying premises in Havelutoo formerly used by Tonga Investment Ltd, is controlled by a five-member charitable trust nominated by the Bahá'í National Assembly, according to Mr Warner.

School fees are $495 a term. Mr Warner said that although that is very expensive compared to the Tongan standard, scholarships and discounts are available for those who cannot afford the fees. To maintain quality, Mr Warner said, the number of students would be kept low, targeting a maximum of 180 students, half of whom would be locals the rest expatriates. He noted that the school compound and facilities could readily accommodate up to 180 students, with rooms for a library and other needs. It also has a tennis court. He said the students would be taught the tenets of all major religions from the Bahá'í belief that all religions have the same mission. By learning about other faiths, students would have the knowledge to choose for themselves when they grow up.

Spiritual virtues are also being taught, said Mr Warner, showing a list of 52 virtues, one of which is to be learned each week. Students should not just become learned but moral, he maintains. "Our objective is not only to have clever children but to have morally good children as well. It's a disaster to have clever but bad ones," he said. And learning spiritual virtues quickens other learning, Mr Warner believes.

Mr Warner, an Australian, owns Warner Islands Line. He resided in Nuku'alofa for 25 years before retiring to his homeland. He has been heavily involved in education in Australia and Indonesia. "Education is my hobby," he said.

Mrs Barbara Hart working with the students at the newly opened Ocean of Light International Primary School in Haveluloto

18
Independent island
nation of Nuie

18
Independent
island nation of Niue

Before leaving the Pacific, I had the misfortune of living on the island of Niue in the 1990s, for reasons I will explain.

But first, picture a large remote rock at latitude 19.02 South and longitude 169.55 West, far from anywhere. Covering 100 square miles, it is one of the largest raised coral atolls in the world surrounded by steep limestone cliffs. The remnants of the population living on the island appropriately nicknamed it the "The Rock". Cook, when he discovered the island in 1774, named it "Savage Island", also very appropriate as he was repelled from landing three times. It was settled in about AD 900 by Polynesians from Samoa and invaded by Tongans in the 16th century. The London Missionary Society followed with their invasion in the 19th century.

The locals and the missionaries persuaded Britain to annex the island in 1889 for fear that another nation (read Tonga) should take possession. A British Protectorate was declared in 1901. Britain gave the unwanted colony to New Zealand to administer, and it became a never-ending administration expense for them. Granting independence to colonies was popular post World War II. New Zealanders thought it would be smart to grant self-government to the Niueans in 1974, but never escaped the increasing costs and demands of the islanders.

Unlike the Polynesians of Tonga and Western Samoa who managed, with help, to control their finances, the Polynesians of Niue became beggars, clinging on to their New Zealand benefactors. A succession of generous New Zealand governments offered, besides money, to give New Zealand citizenship to Niueans, so most of the population packed up and departed to live in New Zealand, supported by the many benefits provided there. Access to free medicine, free education and unemployment benefits were a great attraction. By 1990, it is said that 90–95% of the population lived in New Zealand. The remnants on Niue numbered about 1,400. Abandoned villages were everywhere.

The biggest business and employer in this miniscule independent island nation was government administration. Other funds came from relatives living in New Zealand. Many members of parliament and bureaucrats, disproportional to the population, enjoyed salaries and travel benefits to all manner of conferences worldwide. The budget was financed by New Zealand and whilst the gravy train continued, the remnant population was better off than those of other Pacific nations where most of the population had to work to survive.

Niue was a pleasant quiet place for tourists to have a holiday if one could get there. With the help of aid money, the Government built a second luxury hotel allegedly to attract tourists but also as a pleasant accommodation for overseas experts, policy makers, advisers and consultants who streamed into the little nation to tell them how to run it. Representatives of the United Nations agencies and the International Monetary Fund came to enjoy their travel allowances whilst on exorbitant tax-free salaries. They all had to stay for a minimum one week because there was only one subsidized flight per week to and from Auckland.

I must admit that Niue was not the only place that attracted these unwanted international agencies whose cloistered staff justified a so-called "in depth" study, supported with a jargon-laden report, as an excuse for a tropical junket holiday in luxury accommodation. I thought it hypocritical that they were all obsessed with inequality, but were part of it themselves. But I digress!

Over a period of 25–30 years post-World War II, the continually demanding Niueans had given up their backbone in exchange for a wishbone which was very succulent. Most food was imported and rice became the staple instead of homegrown taro and yams. Farms and food gardens lay idle. The gravy train of family remittances and recurring foreign government aid provided everything to this miniscule nation with a population no bigger than a suburb of Auckland. Strangely, New Zealand has never revolted over this waste.

Post World War II, Part-European Premier Rex, a charming negotiator, orchestrated many of the benefits and wishbones on behalf of his extended family and all Niueans. By the time I arrived, the paternal Premier Rex had died, most of his family moved to New Zealand and his large Alofi trading store had closed.

There remained only two independent trading stores, and one was operated by Burns Philp, the long established island trading company. Starting as a copra buying station in the late 19th century, their assets on the island included a retail store, bakery, copra shed and car agency, all on the main street, and a company staff house elsewhere.

Delicate discharge of beer into the net and onto the barge at Niue 1995

Burns Philp was subject to a takeover in Australia. The new owners were divesting themselves of assets in the Pacific. The price came down and down whilst Burns Philp was conducting fire sales in far flung places. The South Sea history of this company, started in 1870, is an interesting read and can be found in the book *The History of Burns Philp* written by Ken Buckley.

Ross Chapman, the manager of Burns Philp in Tonga, was a good friend of mine and had been given the task of selling the assets of Burns Philp in Niue. Nobody except silly me was interested in buying a business in a potential ghost town.

I saw Niue as a challenge. Would the population stabilize, and could this business expand into growing crops, running livestock and catching fish? The store and facilities would be a good base for expanded activities.

Little did I know that the complicated land tenure laws were to be a handicap to any expansion of rural operations or the long-term retention of building leases. When I thought the price was right, on behalf of my family, I stepped in and bought the Burns Philp business and all its assets in Niue in 1989. It was renamed Niue Trading Co Ltd.

Profits slowly declined under the retained management until I had time to give it more attention in 1993 and 1994. By 1994, serious repairs were needed to the leaking buildings and baking equipment. The lease of the main block was up for renewal, as was the lease on the land occupied by the company house.

Cargo barge and work boat at open anchorage Niue Island 1995

Now I started to realize the many problems associated with land tenure on Niue. Foreigners could not own land. Land was owned by families, represented in the joint names of seven or eight relatives often scattered around the world. Leases had to be signed by all relative members listed on the titles.

Usually one relative remaining on the island fronted to negotiate new leases or renewals on behalf of the owners. It had taken three years for Burns Philp to negotiate the transfer of their lease to Niue Trading Company upon extortionate terms extracted by the absentee owners.

In my investigation into farming land, I had come across this problem and could never get all the signatory owners of any one block to agree. In Vava'u, Tonga, where I had a 32-acre Taro plantation, I only had to deal with one dodgy noble to lease land on his estate. Niue was different. For this reason, and the shortage of workers, I gave up the idea of farming in Niue. I was not entirely disappointed because the land in Niue was not as fertile as that in Tonga. There was only about 6 inches of topsoil over a coral cap base.

Owners no longer worked their farms. As John Steinbeck said in *The Grapes of Wrath*, "They forgot the land, the smell, the feel of it, and remembered only that they owned it." The landowners' representative where the company house was located demanded a huge fee to sign a new lease. The house badly needed repair so I said we would vacate and demolish it if the owners were not open to my counter offer. They tried to call my bluff so we stripped the house and vacated. They had enjoyed power without responsibility.

One cannot blame the Niuean people for the state of affairs. They had become accustomed to not having any interference in their supported way of life. In my opinion, they had given up their backbone in exchange for a wishbone. Recipients of government jobs did not have a hard life, neither did others receiving money from relatives in New Zealand. They had lost their self-esteem and sense of nobility, virtues projected by other Polynesians. Here I was bringing energetic Tongan workers into the country of freeloaders because I could not find local workers.

Amongst others was a hard working capable Tongan lady and her family who ran the company bakery. Jealousy and revenge ensued, and her house was burned down by unknown arsonists whilst she was baking one night. Fortunately, all her kids escaped. Her husband was a crewmember of one of our ships standing by offshore waiting for an opportunity to discharge cargo. He saw the flames of their house burning and swam ashore through rough seas to help.

Frustrated by the declining business and population and not able to start farming, I decided fishing was the next step. This also led to further jealousy and another revenge attack, but the fishing was very interesting whilst it lasted.

Fishing close to Niue was not very rewarding. Trolling for yellowfin tuna was spasmodic and expended a lot of fuel, which was expensive on Niue. Outrigger canoes had taken most of the bottom fish close to the lee cliffs, so offshore fishing was the most attractive.

There were two offshore reefs, namely Beveridge Reef over 200 miles away and Antiope Reef about 180 miles southeast of Niue at latitude 18.15 South, longitude 168.34 West. Antiope Reef never surfaced even at low tide. The coral on the top of this underwater mountain lay about 10 feet under the surface. One could sail over the top of it at high water in a calm sea in a small boat but usually one could see the breakers from three miles away.

Strong currents swirled around the steep undersea mountain as it fell away sharply to great depths. One could drop an anchor on top of the reef and feed out some line to be over 200 fathoms in less than 100 metres from the edge. Needless to say, there were plenty of fish around the unexplored underwater cliffs.

I needed a small seaworthy fishing boat fitted with drop line fishing gear, with a good range. Short of money as usual, in 1993, I bought a second-hand 40-foot plywood launch, which had been clad with a fiberglass skin. Its best attribute was a Gardner 6-cylinder engine out of a truck converted to marine use with a hydraulic gearbox.

With the help of my son who lived in Sydney, we fitted out this launch with large fishing reels and a big icebox lashed on deck. I fell down the hatch whilst doing this and took a few days to recover from the pain, which recurs in my left thigh from time to time. Renamed FV *Ruby*, we shipped it to Tonga on one of our vessels.

The name "Ruby" was chosen because we aimed to catch ruby snapper, shown on the next page. It is a prized fish in Japan and lives a long life in deep waters around underwater mountains in parts of the South Pacific. I did not expect to export any to Japan but aimed to target this variety to substitute imported meats and other protein in Niue.

With a small crew of enthusiastic young Tongans, I sailed it from Tonga to Niue, testing the gear as we went. Because various skills were needed to attack this venture, I skippered the boat for the first few voyages to familiarize the crew with the technique. The days of the GPS (Global Positioning System) had arrived and the crew did not need to be experts in celestial navigation to find this small dot in the ocean. Weather forecasts were studied carefully and the voyages carefully planned, plenty of ice and bait were loaded before departure.

After traveling for about 24 hours, we arrived and started fishing in 180 fathoms, finding large gropers and octopus as well as ruby snapper in the deep water. Some of the gropers must have been 50 years old or more. So heavy were they that we struggled to lift them aboard.

Old groper from 100 fathoms, near Antiope Reef

Crew of FV *Ruby* with ruby snapper

Happy captain with ruby snapper

Drop lining for ruby snapper in 180 fathom, 200 miles east of Niue

An octopus from the deep

Although fitted with four drop-line reels, we found we could only use two at any one time because of the tangles occurring in the strong currents. Each line had a heavy weight and 10 hooks rising from the bottom at intervals of one fathom apart. One could feel the fish biting on our tempting bait, which they must have discovered by smell because there is no light at these depths.

The local fishermen in Niue took great interest and looked at the fish as we loaded them onto the Niue Trading Company truck. Of course the small nation of Niue had a large government fisheries department which was managed by a member of a large fishing family. He wanted to record and weigh all the catch and cross-examined me and the crew in all aspects of the operation. I suspected jealousy was in the air. This was soon confirmed by a sabotage attempt that put an end to my fishing venture.

Because Niue was an unsafe anchorage under the limestone cliffs, I insisted that one of the crew sleep on board and check the anchor from time to time for dragging or drifting too close. We used a heavy anchor then some chain and finally anchor rope to cope with the deep water.

The local fishermen often went diving and spear fishing at night for crayfish and anything that moved. Meanwhile, the virile young Tongan captain had disobeyed my orders and paddled ashore to lay besotted in the arms of a voluptuous local lady. Unattended, the anchor line of FV *Ruby* was cut at the water level and the boat drifted onto the coral shore, badly damaged by the pounding it received.

Although seriously holed, we salvaged the boat but it was never the same. With a sense of defeat, I thought I could never operate a successful business venture in Niue, so eventually the FV *Ruby* was returned to Tonga where there seemed to be more law and order.

The final straw came in negotiating a renewal of the lease of the land upon which the store and other buildings were located. A Niuean who had recently returned to Niue from being a Kings Cross nightclub and casino bouncer in Sydney said he represented the seven signatories of the family who owned the land. He first demanded a higher rent, which I paid and when the time came for renewal, he increased his demands so we went to the lands court.

I had increased the rental payments for the renewed period as set out and required in the written terms of the original lease, but it did not suit him or his bush lawyer who wanted a new lease on new terms. The local judge thought this would be best. We could not agree.

I could not sub-lease any of the vast premises without the landlord's consent. For the two years that I was in residence on the island (1998 and 1999), we argued. The business had shrunk to an unprofitable level. I gave 'licenses to occupy' to the baker, a café, and a movie theatre.

I came to the conclusion that the Niueans on the island were hiding what they really thought and, in the process, hiding the society from genuine scrutiny and assessment. They were clinging to old tribal, sectarian and clannish loyalties—a people of small horizons who close their eyes when they should look. Of course, you meet people like this in many other parts of the world, some not even isolated geographically but in populated countries isolated in their minds and suffering from vague imaginings.

My Australian family were telling me that my pioneering days were over and I should return to Australia where I had purchased a 70-acre block of land on the outskirts of Sydney. Maybe they were right, so Niue became my last active South Pacific adventure and I departed with no desire to return to this island.

The remains of Niue Teaching Co. main building

19
Lessons learned and
farewell to the South Pacific

19
Lessons learned and
farewell the South Pacific

From 1968 to 1999 I learned a few lessons in navigating Pacific life.

One irritating fact is that Government to Government aid is not workable. NGO aid is slightly better when donors offer recipients ways to uplift themselves. Starving people should be given shovels, seeds and fishing lines so they can support themselves with dignity and gain or retain self-esteem. By growing and catching healthy food, one saves both the body and spirit.

Another lesson learned is that besides a piano, the most useless thing on a small ship in a stormy voyage is a seasick passenger. One has to look after them and clean up their mess. Nevertheless, I have observed that they are usually lovely people with many human virtues when you get to know them. Likewise, every large family anywhere in the world includes one or more such passengers, and I mean "passengers for life".

These soft-hearted "passengers for life" are themselves often good at nurturing other family members who may be sick, sad, elderly or very young.

But "passengers for life" cannot handle a job or cope in the outside rough-and-tumble world. We should not be unkind to them if they appear to be lazy or useless because they all serve a purpose in the overall service to mankind. Polynesia has its fair share of these "passengers" but the traditional tribal or extended family unit is familiar and experienced in coping with their welfare. This was so, long before missionaries and "do-gooders" arrived to stir the pot.

Add another virtue to this and an unusual cocktail emerges. I have observed that people living close to nature, who arose from hunters and fishermen into farmers and planters, are very patient, willing to wait a very long time for an opportunity to strike their target. The virtue of patience is not latent in such societies as it is amongst Europeans who are often impatient.

In the 1970s I recall a very strong hurricane that destroyed most of the *fales* (thatched houses) that traditionally were the preferred form of tropical housing in the Ha'apai group. Straight after the destruction the people returned to and rebuilt their shelters in a few days. Plaited together with sennit[1], the roof frames were then thatched with woven coconut leaves.

A foreign aid delegation arrived in Nuku'alofa with the notion of giving small European-type, prefabricated, hurricane proof houses to the victims of the hurricane. One of my fishing boats and I were chartered to take the delegation to the Ha'apai islands to assess their needs.

Word had reached Ha'apai that a bunch of "do-gooders" were heading their way, to provide, free-of-charge, wooden houses with steel roofs to those who wanted them. Before our arrival, the Ha'apai people pushed over and destroyed their newly built *fales* and sat on the beach weeping crocodile tears as we landed.

After presenting the delegation with a humble feast of crayfish and delicious seafood, the islanders apologised for their humble, substandard offering, due to the upheaval and destruction of the hurricane. Eventually, after many months of waiting, everybody acquired a wooden hut. Whilst waiting they rebuilt the *fales*. I mention this as an example of patience and striking when the opportunity comes.

The Niueans adopted the same technique when dealing with the generous New Zealand Governments as explained in the previous chapter. But in so doing they destroyed their self-esteem and the stature of self-reliant nobility, which one observes in other Polynesians.

In the 30-odd years of sailing around and living in the Pacific, I learned that, world-wide, recipients of unearned gratuities lose self-reliance and self-esteem. Their love for one another is thinned with money.

Micronesians in US-controlled islands have lived on green stamp privileges since World War II. By now, most Micronesians have lost all sense of self-reliance. Were they better under the strict rule of the Spanish or Japanese? So-called independence has attracted crooked

---

[1] A type of cordage made by plaiting strands of dried fibre or grass.

politicians and all sorts of carpetbaggers, offering money and deals for a softer life. Thus, the people become hooked on the "benefits of advanced civilization such as canned entertainment and sugary food", which result in obesity and diabetes.

My lessons in the Pacific have been many. Heartaches and disappointments remain with us through our lives. In the ocean of life, obstacles abound that should not be allowed to fester into larger problems. It is only when you run the race that you discover your limitations and abilities. Life on this planet is but a test for the next stage of our eternal voyage.

Finally, I learned how all people—myself included—can adapt to changing circumstances. Islanders are particularly resilient to changes, which are happening faster and faster in this world.

As one matures, one's material needs are less. I observed this particularly amongst the many Polynesians living contented in a well-fed poverty, surrounded by loved ones, music and spiritual enrichment. At the risk of repeating myself, "The measure of a man's wealth is the fewness of his wants."

I am grateful that I departed the Pacific at the turn of the century, a much wiser and a richer person spiritually if not materially.

Appendix 1

THE DROPOUT WHO WENT TO SEA[9]

PETER WARNER, owner of the Tongan trawler which made the Middleton Reef rescue, ran away from his wealthy home at 17 ... and later learned Swedish to sit for his master's certificate. KAY KEAVNEY interviewed him at Ballina.

"I'D PREFER to fight nature rather than human beings," said Peter Warner.

He said it quietly, even with a hint of self-mockery, summing up both himself and his life.

Peter Warner is the now legendary skipper-owner of the Ata, part of his fleet of five fishing boats and two freighters, Tonga-based.

'Ata, the Polynesian name of a certain island, means "the twilight before the dawn."

Earlier that morning, in the milky half light before dawn, Captain Warner had been preparing to bring Ata over the storm-tossed bar into Ballina with the four people from the wrecked yacht *Sospan Fach*.

That bar is dangerous, especially in such weather. First light is one of the few favourable times to cross it.

Peter Warner had radioed from Middleton Reef, 320 miles away, on the preceding Friday that he would cross it precisely then; at first light on this Monday morning.

"And he'll do it," said the old salts in the waiting crowd. "Bang on schedule."

"He's a marvelous sailor," said one.

He did it, bang on schedule, just as the last stars paled. He hadn't even hung about outside, but had timed it exactly, along with doing a little fishing on the long voyage.

In all the madness of the welcome, he'd stayed on his little bridge, unruffled, unfailingly courteous, thick-sweatered, bareheaded, with laughter lines deep-etched round very blue seaman's eyes.

---

[9] Text of article in *The Australian Women's Weekly*—26 June 1974/10 July 1974, page 7.

Now, that night, he was dining by candlelight with photographer Keith Barlow and me in a Ballina restaurant.

He looked urbane in jacket and tie, expertly choosing the wine. This was the other aspect of Peter Warner, privileged son of Sir Arthur Warner, electronics tycoon, former Victorian cabinet minister and Leader of the Upper House on the conservative side.

"I didn't have a tie," he told us, the laughter lines etched deeper. "I tried to borrow one from the (mostly Tongan) crew. The cabin boy was the only one on board who owned one, so I purloined it."

He touched the neat knot.

What drove Peter Warner? What made him tick?

Here was a man who'd tossed it all in to go adventuring, to go to sea, to take off his tie and get away from "getting and spending."

Somewhere, willy-nilly, adventure had kept tapping him on the shoulder.

He had saved so many lives that when, through binoculars, he had spied the *Sospan Fach* survivors on the wrecked Japanese trawler on the reef, he had said to himself, laughing, "Oh no! Not again!"

He poured the wine, and splendid seafood appeared on the candle-lit table, but he chose a thick steak. He'd been living off seafood ever since his three-day voyage to test new fishing equipment changed to a protracted rescue operation.

He was the younger of two brothers, he said, and pretty much the family odd-man-out.

"My brother," he said with affection, "is a scientist, the studious type, the original   absent-minded professor."

Their father, the late Sir Arthur, had many business interests.

Their big home was at Brighton, Victoria, and Peter sailed from as far back as he can remember.

(Later, he had a distinguished career in races like the Hobart Yacht Race, taking line honours in his vessel, Astor, in which he also sailed many thousands of Pacific miles.)

"I was always interested in a physical challenge," he said. "If you like, I was always interested in cowboys and Indians. As a child, I loved the old Viking stories.

"I loved things like boxing and swimming. But I remember giving up boxing, giving it up completely, because I knocked somebody's teeth out."

He paused a while.

"I became fascinated," he went on, "with the study of survival as a youngster, when I tipped over a small sailing boat and stupidly tried to swim ashore. Fortunately, someone had spotted me from the shore, and I was rescued.

"From then on, I studied human survival, both in a practical way and academically. My hobby is still navigating without instruments, using the old ways common in the islands. I love studying the old ships ... and astronomy ...

"When I was 17, I ran away to sea.

"My father caught me when I sailed home a year later, and made me matriculate, then enrol in Law at the University of Melbourne.

"After six weeks of Law I ran away to sea again.

"This time I made it for three whole years. I served in the Swedish and Norwegian navies and fishing fleets. I learnt to speak Swedish ... in fact, I did all my exams for my papers in Swedish.

"After three years I came home sporting my Swedish master's ticket. But my father wanted for me—well, something other than the sea.

"So I asked him, 'What's easiest?'

"My father said, 'Accountancy.' You know, that wasn't true!

"Anyway, for the next five years I worked in his business by day and studied accountancy at night."

Peter eased his tie with a finger.

"Well, after five years of this I was a public accountant, working for my father.

"I had a very broad experience in business.

"But it lost its challenge by the time I was 35. Meanwhile, I'd got married.

"Her name's Justine. She's a beautiful Irish-looking brunette with blue eyes, of Scottish extraction. She was an occupational therapist.

"She's a very good artist, too—in fact, she's a good all-rounder.

"She lived just a few blocks away.

"I explained that no matter what job I did it would involve—" he paused again, choosing his words—"travel. She understood.

"We fixed the date for our marriage. And at once I ran away to sea.

"I explained to Justine that this was my last fling.

"I was away five months and got back two days before the wedding. In my youth I'd worked on Swedish ships doing the Australia-Japan run. And I talked us into a berth on one of these ships—the "hospital" berth—for a honeymoon. It was marvellous. It lasted five months."

Both badly wanted a family, but they were childless for six years.

"Six miscarriages, one after the other," he said very soberly. "Then a premature baby who lived a few days. I couldn't put her through it again. We adopted our much-loved Carolyn, now 13. We owe Carolyn everything. Three months later, Justine was pregnant with Janet (now 11). Peter (now seven) was born in 1966."

Round about 1960, the family had moved from Melbourne to Sydney, with Peter still yoked to business.

"I opened a small fleet of crayfishing boats, based in Tasmania. When I got really fed up with business, I went fishing to regain my sanity.

"I don't mind," he exploded, "fighting villains and thieves and rogues, but not bureaucrats!"

He tugged at the tie.

Year by year, he watched as fields were fished out. Constantly, he searched for new fishing grounds. In this search, in 1966, he sailed one of his, fleet to Tongan waters.

"I was carrying all the latest, most sophisticated European fishing equipment," he said, "but we just couldn't catch those crayfish!

"One day, we had our traps set on a reef about four miles from an uninhabited island called 'Ata.

"Idly, I turned my binoculars on this rugged, volcanic island, and saw a burnt-out patch on a cliff. So in we went to investigate.

"Down the cliff ran a naked youth. Others followed, yelling. They were so wild that the crew started looking at our guns."

In this first famous rescue, he restored to their parents six schoolboys (still ranging only from 14 years to 18) from Tonga, who had purloined a boat 15 months before for a night's illicit fishing and been carried away by storms.

They fascinated the student of survival.

"Two of the elder youths emerged as natural leaders, holding absolute sway over the others. All societies seem to begin like that, with the emergence of born aristocrats."

Later, some of the boys joined his crew. One, Mano Totau (of whom young Peter Lindenmayer was to say, "Mano's the hero. He saved us"), was part of the *Sospan Fach*'s rescue party.

In Tonga, Peter Warner was feasted and feted.

And every feast happened to sport lavish helpings of crayfish. The islanders had succeeded where others with all their fishing equipment had failed!

In gratitude to the savior of their sons and heirs, the Tongans promised to share the secrets of their fishing grounds and methods.

Then Peter approached his wife about moving to Tonga.

So the Warners moved to Tonga (though keeping their Cammeray, Sydney, house). They live near the royal palace.

Justine learnt to love the life.

"Pretty soon," Peter said, "she was running the local art society, and the Red Cross, and the bridge clubs, and setting up the first bookshop in Tonga."

Peter junior could swim like a fish almost before he could walk.

"For years," said his father, "his was the only white bottom among the brown ones."

Adventure, for little Peter, first meant sneaking into the royal palace nearby.

By then, Queen Salote was dead, and her successor was the Queen Consort, Maataho, very stately and well over 6 ft. tall.

"Around then, I'd been trying to teach Peter the difference between truth and a lie.

"This morning, when he was all of three, he got away from his Tongan nanny, sneaked past the guards, and got into the palace, and ran right into the stately queen.

"She said, 'Who are you?'"

"He said, 'I'm Peter Warner. Who are you?'"

"Her Majesty said, 'I am Queen Maataho.'

"And, Peter looked up at her and barked. 'Truth or a lie?'"

This year, young Peter and his sunbrowned sisters—with their mother—have gone back to the Cammeray house to be educated in Australian schools.

As often as he can, Peter Warner flies home to Sydney, as he did this month. Then, on to Ballina and the Richmond River, where Ata (named after the island of that first rescue operation) was being reconverted as a fishing vessel.

What now for Peter Warner?

In answer, Peter talked of his beloved Polynesians. "They love and know the sea as few Europeans do. Theirs are undeveloped countries. My present dream is to develop the Polynesian sea-farming capabilities into a Norway of the Pacific," he said.

"I think the Polynesians can become the seafarers and harvesters of the Pacific."

Appendix 2

Correspondence

Ocean of Light education

PRIMARY SCHOOL

P. O. Box 2878
Nukualofa,
TONGA,
South West Pacific

Ph. (676) 21174
Fx. (676) 23120

Office of Social & Economic Development,   19 January 1998
Bahá'í World Centre
Haifa,
Israel

Dear Friends,

Overview of first 2 years of
Ocean of Light Primary School
in Kingdom of Tonga

For the benefit of worldwide friends who are contemplating starting Bahá'í academic schools, we thought we should share with you some of the success and problems encountered in Tonga during the two 2 years of operation. Your office may be able to disseminate information to communities where appropriate.

In March 1996, the Bahá'í community in Tonga were blessed with the approval from the Government of Tonga to open a Bahá'í Primary School in the capital of Nukualofa. The NSA of Tonga incorporated a Trust to conduct the school. The Trustees are appointed by the NSA.

Before the decision to commence the school was made, deep consideration was given to the guidelines and self-examination questions distributed by your office concerning the opening of Bahá'í schools. We believe all the potential problems were covered but found it necessary to adopt a novel approach to the finance question, because the NSA of Tonga had and has no funds to support the school.

Because the only Government run English-speaking school was and is overcrowded, the opportunity existed to enrol foreign and some local children from affluent families, who wish their children to have an early grounding in the English language. Consequently, we were and are able to charge fees to this sector of the community, comparable to the other International schools in nearby countries. This is the first international standard, multi-cultural, bi-lingual school in Tonga. It costs money to run a school of excellence and the fees reflect this.

However there are many poor local Bahá'í and non Bahá'í families who do not have the cash to pay these fees, and we are reminded of the advice given by the Guardian on 9 July 1931 to an individual:

"Let them freely and without charge, open the doors of Bahá'í schools to non-Bahá'í children who are poor and in need."

To cover this aspect, and to keep an even balance of local and foreign students in the school, we launched a scholarship drive to individual friends and to LSA's in Australia, New Zealand and California. A copy of a sample self-explanatory request letter is enclosed. To date we have been blessed with reasonable results from this circular but mainly from LSA's who donate less than one scholarship. Nevertheless overall, we can combine these part donations into full or nearly full scholarships. We have also encouraged the poor parents of scholarship students to contribute something towards their child's fees. A small contribution lifts their sense of participation and self-esteem. Our campaign for scholarships continues and expands so that we can both run a school of excellence and at the same time keep the doors open for poor and needy.

It is the prayer of the Trustees that ultimately this primary school will expand into three divisions, namely the primary school, a high school of which two classes will commence in 1998 and finally a vocational school. However we must first develop the character and polish the virtues of the young pupils, before they can advance into the intense hard work of higher education. We are guided by the tablet of Abdul-Baha, Vol. III, pp. 578–9 which explains

"It is extremely difficult to teach the individual and refine his character once puberty is passed."

The primary motive of establishing the school is of course to educate the children and the second motive is to propagate the Faith. We had observed the success of Christian sects in multiplying their believers by establishing and operating their own schools. The attending children teach their parents and family the religious lessons learned in these schools, thereby attracting many new believers overall. Although the school day starts with a Bahá'í prayer and virtues studies, we only teach the Bahá'í Faith with words in the comparative religion course. Our desire is to acquaint students and their families with the Faith presented to them in a non-threatening atmosphere where seekers may naturally ask questions.

We concluded that a most cost effective and long-term satisfactory method of expanding the Faith is to educate the next generation. Some of us sincerely believe that most of the Bahá'í worldwide resources should be concentrated on education of the young.

The Ocean of Light School opened with only 9 pupils. In the second year we reached 52 students. At the start of the third year we have 75 enrolments. This slow start bas given us the needed time to train staff, iron out material problems and test all the Bahá'í and other progressive methods of teaching, always keeping to the basic curriculum laid down by Government regulations. The Government requirements in Tonga emphasise the importance of reading writing and arithmetic. It also requires the teaching of science and social science. All of this fits well with Bahá'í education ideas. Otherwise Government policies leave open opportunities to teach other things by other means. Some of these are as follows.

(1) The Virtues Program has been adopted and encouraged on a changing weekly theme but participated by all on a daily basis, and running throughout all subjects.

(2) Exercises in co-ordinating both the left and right band side of the brain have helped progress.

(3) Making school a joyful experience with song and play and other activities has created good self-esteem amongst students.

(4) Physical education every day is considered important for development of "the throne of the inner temple". Non-competitive sport has been successful amongst the younger pupils.

(5) Caring is encouraged between age groups by having young children read to older children and visa-versa. This is also demonstrated when Tongan children teach their language to foreign pupils and English speaking children teach their language to the Tongans.

(6) Peer tutoring bas been encouraged with success. Faster learning children assist slower learning pupils and at the same time cement their own lessons by teaching others.

These are some of the small success areas.. We are blessed with the opportunity to adopt all the modern Bahá'í techniques which we are practising.

A conference of Pacific based Bahá'í educators was held in August 1997 at the school, which attracted participants from Western Samoa, Japan, Korea, New Zealand and Australia. More ideas were learned as a result of this conference where many subjects were shared.

That concludes our short report, but we would like to add a suggestion for the consideration of your office and the Universal House of Justice.

Governments of both advanced and developing countries are insisting that primary school teachers have a minimum academic qualification of Diploma of Education, or equivalent. This is normally a course involving 2 or 3 years in a college plus probationary teaching in one or more schools.

At the January 1996 conference of Bahá'í educators in Auckland, representatives from many Bahá'í academic schools from around the Pacific attended. After consultation most of us expressed concern at the lack of qualified Bahá'í teachers in the world. Soon there will be many more Bahá'í academic schools throughout this region and the problem of lack of teachers will multiply.

In Australia and New Zealand, there are sufficient PhD qualified Bahá'í educators to staff and run a Bahá'í Teachers Training College. From a background of teaching in a Western fashion, many would have to re-learn, accept and apply themselves to a paradigm shift needed to absorb the most progressive Bahá'í methods and approaches.

We pray that you may keep this idea of a Pacific teachers training college in mind. Perhaps some of the course could be conducted at the partly used Yerrinbool school in Australia and the practical experience achieved at the Ocean of Light School in Tonga. We cannot offer much but our facility and humble skills are to be shared by the friends in education worldwide.

With loving Bahá'í wishes
[signed]
Barbara Hart
Principal

[signed]
Peter Warner
Trustee

Appendix 3

Correspondence regarding the two Niuas

Summary of suggestions to boost development of the two Niuas
Submitted by Peter Warner to Government of Tonga, August 1996

(1) Declare Niuafo'o in addition to NTT (Niuatoputapu) as a "Port of Entry" for visiting vessels and aircraft. This would encourage cargo, fishing vessels and yachts to visit whilst en route to other ports

(2) Declare both Niuas as duty free ports, free from port and service tax and duty (GST to remain) to encourage (a) small foreign and Tongan fishing vessels to use NTT as a base for fueling, provisioning, and repairing vessels and gear. (b) visits from foreign yachts and (c) trade in general.

(3) Using foreign aid money, improve infrastructure—Roads, Water storage, Harbour facilities, but not Power, see (5) below

(4) Project ecological image of organic food supplies exported from two pollution free islands. This would be particularly encouraging for Niuafo'o taro growers.

(5) Promote alternative energy. Offer development licenses and Development Bank loans to those wishing to establish "stand alone" alternative power sources and energy saving devices.

(6) Grant development licenses to foreign organizations in fields which boost the local economy, particularly fishing, fish processing, agriculture, accommodation and food processing.

(7) At diplomatic level, massage relationships with Western Samoa, and Wallis and Futuna, to encourage trade and fishing cooperation between the two Niuas and these nearby neighbours. Joint ventures should be encouraged.

(8) After implementing item (2) above, withdraw the monopoly shipping subsidy, because shipping companies will then be encouraged to enhance competitive services.

(9) Push the Ministry of Labour and Commerce to speedily process development license applications in order to lift the bureaucratic dead hand of Government presently in place.

CPSIA information can be obtained
at www.ICGtesting.com
Printed in the USA
BVHW071228290421
606134BV00006B/782